BLAC
SCIENTISTS & INVENTORS™
IN THE UK

Millenniums of Inventions & Innovations

Michael Williams
and
Manyonyi Amalemba

BLACK SCIENTISTS & INVENTORS™ IN THE UK

Millenniums of Inventions & Innovations

Michael Williams &
Manyonyi Amalemba

Design and layout: Cindy Soso

BIS Publications 2015

BIS Publications

First Printing: November 2014
Second Printing January 2015

ISBN 9781903289273

BIS Publications
www.bispublications.com
www.blackscientistandinventors.com

Tel: 07903 791 469

Ordering Information:

Special discounts are available on quantity purchases
by corporations, associations, educators, and others.
For details, contact the publisher at the above listed address.
Trade bookstores and wholesalers:

Please contact BIS Publications
Tel: +44(0)7903 791 469
or email: info@bispublications.com

A catalogue record for this book exists in the British Library.

DISCLAIMER:

Whilst every effort has been made to provide accurate information, neither the authors or the publisher shall have liability to any person or entity with respect to any errors, omissions or inaccuracies contained herein.

Dedication

- The Freedom Fighters of the Caribbean & Africa, who sacrificed their lives so that future generations could be free.
- The enslaved Africans who tolerated all forms of humiliation in order to fight another day so that we could see today.
- Those Africans that came to help Britain through both World Wars I and II and lets not forget the Black loyalist of 1775 –1783 in the American War of Independence.
- The Windrush Generation.
- Those who conquered their fears and came to the UK during the 40s, 50s and 60s and fought for equal rights so that my generation could have a better life.
- To my parents [Williams] who did all they could to give their children a better life.
- To the family Amalemba for sticking together through some very rough times.
- Those that believed in this project and helped make it happen.

All people regardless of Race & Gender who Seek ***TRUTH.***

Acknowledgements

Michael Williams

First of all, I would like to give thanks and gratitude to the Master Scientist, Inventor and Creator of all things. To Cindy Soso who believed in this project from the start and got behind both authors, with support, encouragement and personal sacrifice. I would like to thank all those that have supported the Black Scientists and Inventors series of books, greeting cards, posters, poster packs, and presentations, since 1997 until now. It is my hope that the topic of Black Scientists and Inventors is not relegated to just Black History Month, October in UK and February in the rest of the world, or just included in schools as supplementary reading. My hope and my aim is that it's included as part of the school curriculum, where everyone is encouraged to learn about these very significant and life changing contributions.

Manyonyi S. Amalemba

I would like to thank Michael Williams CEO of BIS Publications for affording me the opportunity to indulge myself and to share with you some of the most inspiring people I have ever come across. The scientists you will read about in these pages are just some of the many unsung heroes that have- and for some are still- representing at the highest level in their chosen fields. I acknowledge all those that get a mention herein, but more so those others that still go unnoticed but continue to forge on, regardless.

CONTENTS

CONTENTS

"GOD and Nature [Thought] first made us what we are, and then out of our own created genius we make ourselves what we want to be. Follow always that great law. Let the sky and God be our limit and Eternity our measurement."

The Most Honourable Marcus Mosiah Garvey.

CONTENT PAGE SCIENTISTS & INVENTORS

INTRODUCTION

This title is the 5th in the best-selling Black Scientists and Inventors series of books. I chose to focus on just scientists, inventors, innovators, medics and engineers of African descent who were born in the UK, educated in the UK, or spent most or part of their working lives in the UK. The reason I focused on UK talented people was because too often I've found that both teachers and students were unaware of the magnificent contributions that black people have made to the historical and contemporary scientific landscape of the UK. This is one of the reasons why I believe the African contribution has been omitted from the school curriculum.

In this volume I was blessed to have the assistance of Manyonyi Amalemba, author of Becoming and who co-authors this title. He brings to this work his decades of experience as a mentor, educator and coach of children and young people in the UK.

It is our hope that both adults and children of all cultures in general and those of African descent in particular are inspired by this book to go on and continue contributing to the scientific development of this country and the world in general. To this end we hope that the inspiring stories within these pages give both adults and young people examples to aspire towards, which in turn will create a new generation of Dr Harold Moody, Professor Charles Ssali, Francis Williams, Dr. Margaret Aderin-Pocock, Dr Geoff Palmer, Leeroy Brown, Peter Sesay and Dr. Eyman Osman, just to name a few.

PREFACE

A Brief History of Briton From 8,000 B.C.E. to 1960s The contributions from people of African descent to Britain, is anything but new. Africans have been contributing to the UK since the earliest of times. There have been many waves of Africans immigrating to the UK over millenniums. The earliest times would be when man rose from the cradle of civilization in central east Africa and millenniums later migrated throughout the entire world and this included Britain. The second entry into Britain were the people we refer to now as ancient Britons or Iberian Celt (Black Celts) who walked the British shores around 8,000 B.C.E.

The third came with the Roman conquest of Britain around 79 C.E., and the occupation of it in 197 C.E. by Emperor Septimius Severus, who was an African.

Around 700 C.E. Africans can once again be seen in numbers in Britain, they were referred to as Black

Moors, Blackamoore or just Moors. These Africans again having a huge impact on the British historical landscape by leaving their culture which still effects us all today. One example of this is Morris dancing usually performed in the North of England. There is also evidence that it was the Moors who brought the bagpipes from Spain to Scotland.

The fifth wave of Africans was during the Tudor times 1457-1509, at first not as slaves but free people engaged in trade and commerce. An example is 'Blacke Trumpet' John Blanke was a musician who played in the court of Henry the VII and Henry the VIII for a salary of £20.00 per month.

The sixth was in the 1700s, when a large group of enslaved and free Africans fought alongside the British during the American War for Independence. The enslaved Africans were promised freedom, financial compensation and resettlement in England as a reward for their help. - It must be noted that they did not receive any financial compensation and became part of the Black poor in London.

One would think that after the cruel treatment, which Africans suffered during the "Trans-Atlantic Enslavement Trade", they would stay clear of Europe and Europeans. Not so, in the early 1900s and 1940s there was a seventh migration of Africans who came to Britain's aid to help keep Britain free from Nazi occupation during the First and Second World Wars. These Africans from the West Indies along with their African American brothers --who incidentally suffered under the same western European slavery system -- came to Britain volunteering their services to help, what they thought, was their mother country in her time of great need.

Within these pages you will discover how Africans from the continent of Africa and its diaspora are continuing what their ancestors did in the past and that is positively contributing to the social and wider fabric of Britain. There by helping her maintain her place on the global map despite Britain's "Colour Bar", prejudices and racial discrimination of Africans in Britain in the preceding centuries. Herein are poignant examples of perseverance, staying power and achievements against all odds and adversaries.

Michael Williams, 2014.

Something Inside So Strong - I'll Make It although you Do me So Wrong!

"The higher you build your barriers
The taller I become
The farther you take my rights away
The faster I will run

Something inside so strong
I know that I can make it

Tho' you're doing me wrong, so wrong
Brothers and sisters
When they insist we're just not good enough
When we know better
Just look 'em in the eyes and say
I'm gonna do it anyway...

...Something inside so strong."

Labi Siffre

Part I: Chapter 1 -

On Why This is Not Taught In Schools & The Great Cover Up

CHAPTER 1

On Why This is Not Taught In Schools and the Great Cover Up

To really appreciate the significance of the contributions people of African descent have made and continue to make to Britain or the United Kingdom (U.K.), we have to put them into historical context; that is, to tell a story of African resistance, self-reliance, inventiveness, innovativeness and creativity in its historical relationship with whites, in the Caribbean, the Americas, Africa and the UK. For this reason we have not written just a book on the subject of African achievements in science, medicine, inventions and innovations, although that alone would enlighten us to the herculean contributions Africans have made to the UK. That publication may have already been written and if not we leave space for others to complete. In this title we examine African achievements in the context of the extreme difficulties they faced whilst making these huge contributions. With this understanding it gives us a whole new perspective and reverence towards our fore-fathers who are paragons for us all today.

A Crime of Omission and Commission

Let's first start with why most of us reading this book will be finding out this information for the very first time. And why to this very day (May 1st 2014) in most UK schools and schools of former and current British colonies, the content of this publication is not taught in classrooms, which incidentally is both a crime of omission and commission. It's our belief that the UK educational system, or rather training of young people, is directly connected to the control of wealth and resources; and that this control is being exercised by very few people. Notice we say training and not education, as the two are very different. Anyone can be trained to mimic what the trainer is showing them, even animals, and so this is not an education; we state what we believe education is later. It is very true that information, knowledge and know-how are truly powerful and can transform a life. The problem with this is that there are those who would deny this education to 95% of the world's population, reason being fear of competition and the decrease of their overall control of the planets resources. They have been known to use physical force, as in military might, but even more significantly mental force, which is where education/training comes into play, in order to maintain the status quo.

The School System

The current UK national school system was born in 1860s and 1880s. Before this in feudal England most people, including children, worked as subsistence farmers producing enough food for themselves; any extra they would take to market and sell. This is known as the agrarian age. Due to wealth that was created from the Caribbean during the trans-Atlantic Enslavement Trade, Britain's coffers were over-flowing with money and much of this money was invested in the country's infrastructure, inventors, inventions and new mechanical machinery. It helped give birth to the industrial revolution. However, these mechanical devices that could do the work of 10, 20 or 100 men and women created a problem in that there weren't enough skilled people to operate them. The current (state) school system was created to solve this problem by training the masses with the purpose of creating functional workers who could operate machinery at the onset of the industrial revolution. The schooling system was never created for people to be able to think for themselves, but really for people to do what they are told. A part of correct thinking is to have correct truthful information at the base of correct thoughts-without this people are left in a state of confusion.

A Good Education Is Worth More Than Silver Or Gold

Contrary to popular belief that African people don't enjoy reading and writing, this could not be further from the truth as Africans have always valued education. In fact, if one studies the history of African people, education ranks highly, well before material possessions. Education and African spiritual beliefs were intertwined; they built temples, universities and libraries in reverence to education. When they travelled to other parts of the world they tried to civilize other people by imparting both local and universal knowledge to them. Even during the terrible episode of the trans-Atlantic Enslavement Trade, Africans in the Caribbean and the Americas would risk their own lives trying to secretly learn how to read and write.

Today, are we receiving the right type of education?

In order to answer this question let's first look at two things. First, what is education? If we break down the etymology of the word education we find that at its root, it's derived from the Latin word "educo", which means "I rise up" or "I bring out." So we can see that the true meaning of education is to bring out of a person what already exists and not to put into a person.

A good example of what an education is not can be found in the book 'Outwitting The Devil'. Best-selling author Napoleon Hill says

> *"Children in schools around the world are taught and encouraged not to THINK, but to adopt other people's ideas and thoughts" .*[1]

So are our young people today receiving an education?

Well what good is an education if after you receive it you can't sustain yourself, family or community? Today black children in the UK are attending all types of universities from the very worst to the very best. But after graduation many of them are finding themselves disproportionately unemployed and many of them are just languishing at home doing very little. The question is should that be accepted as the norm or should we be looking at it as an opportunity to make real positive change in a young black person's life?

If we study African American educationalists and industrialist Booker T. Washington, Washington created a university to teach black people, who at the time were just emancipated from enslavement, how to use their own hands and intellect to build businesses within their communities, that would sustain them and even flourish. A great example of this type of education was the famous business area in Tulsa, Oklahoma USA during the 1900s, called the Black Wall Street. Ex-enslaved Africans were left alone to create and build, which they did and within a few years of Emancipation, they flourished. Perhaps from our historical experiences, we could use these positives stories to help our young people move forward today.

How to Get a Good Education

The leader of the Universal Negro Improvement Association (UNIA), the Hon Marcus Mosiah Garvey, in his writings 'Message To The People - The Course of African Philosophy' Garvey says:

> *"...You must never stop learning. The world's greatest men and women were people who educated themselves outside the university with all the knowledge that the university gives, you have the opportunity of doing the same as the university student does, read and study. One must never stop reading; read everything that you can read, that is of standard knowledge..."* [2]

> *"..Use every spare minute you have in reading. If you are going on a journey that would take an hour carry something with you to read for that hour until you have reached*

> *the place. Read through at least one book every week separate and distinct from newspapers and journals. It will mean that at the end of one year you will have then read 52 different subjects. After 5 years you will have read over two hundred and fifty books. Never forget that intelligence rules the world and ignorance carries the burden."* [3]

Garvey goes on to say that *"There is nothing in the world that you want that you cannot have so long as it's possible in nature and men have achieved it before..."* [4]

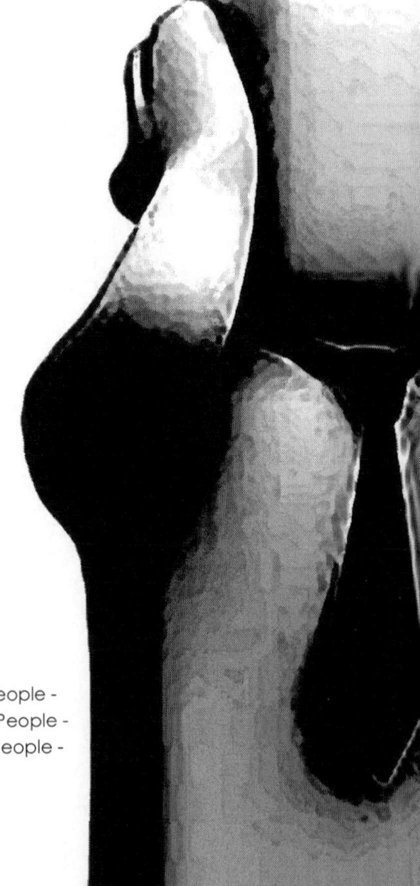

Notes & References

1. Out Witting The Devil, Napoleon Hill | 2. Message To The People - The Course of African Philosophy, Pg 1 | 3. Message To The People - The Course of African Philosophy, Pg 7 | 4. Message To The People - The Course of African Philosophy, Pg 9.

Part I:
Chapter 2 -
Blatant Lies

CHAPTER 2

Blatant Lies

Most of us confuse opinions with facts, falsehood with truth, and belief with science. African American psychiatrist Joy Degruy has found that most people believe that if something is written in a book then most people believe that it must be true. Little do they know that not all that's written in a book is true or correct. Sometimes the book's contents may just be the author's opinion, theory or hypothesis. The opinion, theory or hypothesis may be correct but it may also be incorrect. That's not a problem, but it becomes dangerous when the reader believes that it is a fact.

What is a belief? According to Collins English Dictionary, a belief is:

> "An opinion, principle, accepted as true, often without proof."

Then what is science? In the same dictionary, science is:

> "A systematic study and knowledge of natural or physical phenomena."

What is a fact? According to Wikipedia a fact is:

> "...something that has really occurred or is actually the case."

Whilst we are on this point I may as well define what a lie is. Collins defines it as:

> "Make a deliberately false statement, a deliberate intent to deceive or an intentional untruth."

So, it is important that when we read books we recognize whether what the writer has written is fact or just a theory, hypothesis or his opinion. I say this because many books written by European writers about African people are not based on fact but on their personal opinions. Also some European scientists who have written about Africans have called their conclusions facts and science, when at best, they are just their theories and at worst, their own personal beliefs. Some European writers during the 18th and 19th centuries wrote many lies about people of African descent, and many of them tried to use some form of pseudo-science to prove their theory. This was mainly done in order to support the argument that the black man was to work for the white man and that it was the white man's duty to civilize the black man from an animal state. Many theories were concluded by these scientists, such as the 18th century eminent biologist, Carl Von Linnaeus, who tried to classify races of man in a system he developed.

Linneaus, a Swedish naturalist and botanist, was born in 1707; he is famed for establishing the scientific method of naming plants and animals. In his system, which is called Taxonomic, each living (organism) thing has two parts. They are the genus (group) and the species (kind). It is the genius and species that make up the organism's scientific name, for example the scientific name for modern humans is Homo sapiens, where Homo is the genus and sapiens the kind. In this system plants and animals are grouped in the following way: Cow and Oxen are bovine, Douglas firs, giant sequoias and redwoods are all conifers. Panthers, tigers, jaguars and leopards are all felines, all bovine and felines are mammals etc.[1]

In her book Post Traumatic Slave Syndrome, Degruy postulates that:

> *"The problem with Linnaeus system is that he tried to expands his theory in order to define different 'types' of humans, and unlike all his previous work he classified humans using considerably fewer objective descriptions. With this highly suspect effort to classify humans, Linnaeus began the science of anthropology and laid the foundation for 19th century beliefs about race that resulted in racism."*[2]

How Linnaeus categorized race can be found in J.S. Haller's book 'Outcast From Evolution'. Linnaeus describes: [3]

- Homo Americanus as reddish, choleric, obstinate, contented and regulated by customs

- Homo Asiaticus as sallow, grave dignified, avaricious, and ruled by opinion; and Homo Afer as black, phlegmatic, cunning, lazy, lustful, careless, and governed by caprice.

Johann Friedrich Blumenbach continued from were Linnaeus left off.[4] Blumenbach a German physician, naturalist, physiologist, and anthropologist was born in 1752. His teachings in comparative anatomy were applied to the classification of what he called human races, of which he determined there to be five.[5]

In his treatise 'On the Natural Variety of Mankind', he developed his own system of human classification, which was the Caucasian, Mongolian, American, Ethiopian, and Maylan races. His classification was based on skin colour, hair type, skull and phenotype. Out of his five varieties of man he placed the Caucasian at the top - incidentally a name he derived from Mount Caucus which is located near the eastern borders of Turkey and western part of Russia. Blumenbach believed that Caucasians were the first humans and he qualified this with pseudo-science. In this quote we learn how he arrives at this conclusion

> "...it is white in colour [skull], which we may fairly assume to have been the primitive colour of mankind."[6]

Although this was only Blumenbach's opinion as there was no science used in his assumptions, this opinion was treated as fact and was used to shape the mind of European scholars during the 18th and 19th centuries and to some degree, even to this day. But more to the point both Linnaeus' and Blumenbach's opinions had helped to ease the guilt of those involved in the dehumanization and trauma of a people during the trans-Atlantic enslavement process.

Some of the negative propaganda that was being used against the African at that time was:

Carl Linnaeus

Johann Friedrich Blumenbach

Carl Linnaeus

Edward Long

Thomas Carlyle

- As the African skull is smallest of all the three groups of Human beings [Linnaeus], he therefore must have the smallest brain. (Phrenology).
- The African is born to labour and he does not feel pain either physically or mentally to the degree of the Caucasian.
- The African woman is always sexually ready.
- The African is capricious.[7]

Some European scholars used the above theories on most people of colour but more so on the African in order to justify his enslavement and colonization. For example, it was used during the transatlantic enslavement period to justify the forceful removal of the native people of the Americas from their land which resulted in a genocide of people as far north as Canada, and as far south as Argentina and across the Caribbean region; then to forcefully move millions of African people from African countries to the Americas. And let's forget the forced movement of aboriginal people from their lands in Australia, New Zealand, and other Pacific islands. In fact the native people of Tasmania were completely wiped off the island by European invaders.[8] Here we see racist theories being used again, according to English author Edward Long, in his two volume book 'History of Jamaica', first published in 1774 and again in 1970. Some have said that it's a classic but the book contains many racist overtones. Long argues that the American Negroes are characterized by the same "bestial manners, stupidity and vice which debase their brethren in Africa." He goes on to say that "...these groups of people embody every species of inherent turpitude and imperfection, these people have no redeeming qualities whatsoever." [9]

Long uses this type of language in his writings to undermine black scientist, mathematician and educator, Francis Williams as well as the education of black people more widely. Noting that Williams had established a school in Spanish Town, Jamaica, he suggested that a black pupil had been sent "mad", where "the abstruse problems of mathematical intuition turned his brain." He used this as an example to put across his racist belief that "every African head is not adapted by nature to such profound contemplations". Long goes on to attack Williams personally, arguing that

> "...he was haughty, opinionated, looked down with foreign contempt on his fellow Blacks", as well as accusing him of "cruelty".[10]

In December 1849, in Fraser's Magazine famous English author Thomas Carlyle a personal friend of Charles Dickens, wrote a piece entitled 'Occasional Discourse on the Negro Question.' In the piece Carlyle writes

> "The perfect society would have the wisest man ruling absolutely at the top, the next wisest in the next position of power, and so on, with the Negroes at the bottom, just above the domestic animals."

He goes on to say that

> "The white race was born wiser than the black race, and thus to emancipate Negroes was only to deprive them of their God given master". (Freeman & Griffin: 2002)

Lies, More Lies & the Great Cover Up

Donald B. Griffin co-author of 'Return To Glory' recites what Dr Chancellor Williams said were several tactics employed by western anthropologists to blot out African accomplishment. Below is the list:

1. "Ignore or refuse to publish any facts of African history" that would not support their racial theories.

2. "Create a religious and 'scientific'doctrine" to ease the white conscience for oppressing and enslaving African people.

3. "Flood the world with hastily thrown together African 'histories'" that contain European perspectives only.

4. "Start renaming people and places. Replace African names of persons, places, and things with Arabic and European names." This will disguise their true black identity.

5. Change the criteria for defining race. For example, one drop of Negro blood in America makes you a Negro, no matter how light your skin. When reporting ancient history, reverse the standard. Make one drop of white blood render someone a Caucasian no matter how dark the skin.

6. When black participation in civilization is so obvious your best schemes can't hide it, find a way to attribute the success to outside white influence.

7. When all the ancient historians contradict your theory, seek to discredit them.

Since the ancient historians, as mentioned earlier, describe the Egyptians, Syrians, Sumerians and Phoenicians, as black folk, new definitions were required. The anthropologists decided black skin, thick lips, woolly hair, and broad noses were insufficient data to make a person an African. So they created a new man, a dark skinned white man with woolly hair.[11]

As can be seen of the so called discourse amongst the elite, ideas and opinions were put forward by some of the most eminent brains/scholars of the time no less, to produce negative propaganda on the question of race in order to propagate the same. No scientific methodology to underpin their proposals at all. The utterances, personal opinions and purposeful racist writings were not questioned and would never be questioned. All taken as fact! As alluded to herein belief versus fact? Who cared they did the job.

Notes & References

1. Post Traumatic Slave Syndrome, J. Degruy, pg 59. | 2. ibid pg 59 / 3. ibid pg 60 / 4. ibid pg 60 / 5. http://en.wikipedia.org/wiki/Johann_Friedrich_Blumenbach | 6. Post Traumatic Slave Syndrome, J. Degruy, pg 61. | 7. ibid pg 65-69. | 8. Our Story, J.H Clarke, | 9. http://en.m.wikipedia.org/wiki/Edward_Long#History_of_Jamaica | 10. The Royal Society, 2012, web page. | 11. Return to Glory, Freeman & Griffin 2002, pg 80.

Part II: Chapter 3 -

It All Started with Africans the Inventors of the first Civilizations

Dr. Chancellor Williams

CHAPTER 3

It All Started with Africans the Inventors of the First Civilizations

Let's first start at the beginning. When scientists search for man's genesis they may start by looking in Europe, Asia, or the Americas but any serious scientists and scholars during this research will always end up in Africa. The reason for this is that the oldest human bones which scientists have discovered have been in East African countries such as Lake Turkana in Kenya, Hada in Ethiopia, Kagera River in Uganda and Olduvai Gorge in Tanzania.[1]

The scientists Mary and Louis Leaky carried out extensive research in the region during the 1930s. According to their findings and other scientists who followed on from their research, a type of ape-like man or Hominid's bones, have been found and have been dated to as far back as 6 million years. They named him Orrorin tugenensis. About 3.9 million years ago lived another type of Hominid- they called him

Australopithecus Africanus. There were several types since then that lived in Africa which include 'Lucy', found in Ethiopia, who lived around 2.8 million years ago, up until Homo erectus who lived some 1.8 million years ago and was given that name because he was the first to walk upright. The discovery at Olduvai Gorge, Tanzania dates back some 2 million years. They gave him the name Zinjanthropus, which translates to 'East African man'. Modern man Homo-sapiens (sapiens) is thought to have evolved from the Hominid genus preceding around 150,000 - 250,000 years ago.[2]

How Man Populated the Earth – Theory 1

After approximately 6 million years Africans moved from east central Africa to all corners of the continent. Scientist have now deduced that at one time the world was one mass all joined together. It was called Pangaea with Africa at its centre, and it's because of moving plates under the earth that we now have separate land masses, which we call continents. So it follows if human beings existed on the planet at that time, travel to America, China, Australia and Europe would have been quite possible - even without getting their feet wet. These Africans that travelled throughout the world would have been the original people in those lands. Although this is just a theory and some reading this will immediately reject the possibility simply because of what they have always been taught, we would suggest at least entertain the idea by carrying out your own independent research first.

Theory 2

There is solid evidence which shows Africans travelled throughout the world again around 45000 BC, after the last European Ice age. They most likely travelled into Europe via North Africa across the Gibraltar Straits and into the Iberian Peninsula. These were a genus (group) of people European anthropologists called Grimaldi man - most likely the Khoi and San people - who travelled from the southern tips of Africa to the north, into southern Europe and as far east as Siberia in Russia and even northern Europe. As they travelled they left paintings on cave walls that remind us that they were there first. Some of these reminders can be found in a place in Italy called Grimaldi, hence the name Grimaldi man, given to the African.

They may have also been the first humans to travel to the Americas. An article in the New York Times dated March, 27th 2014, reads:

> "Dr Guidon, Brazilian professor of Archaeology shows similar paintings to those that were found in European caves now found in a Brazilian cave."

The article goes on to say

> "...Dr. Guidon remains defiant about her findings. At her home on the grounds of a museum she founded to focus on the discoveries in Serra da Capivara, she said she believed that humans had reached these plateaus even earlier, around 100,000 years ago, and might have come not overland from Asia but by boat from Africa."[3]

In 1869 in Mexico in Central America, Jose Meglar a Mexican scholar wrote in the National Society of Geography and Statistics Bulletin that a few years earlier (1862) he was in San Andres where he had been taken to see a Colossal Head. He said

> *"...I was struck with surprise. As a work of art, it is without exaggeration a magnificent sculpture. What astonished me was the Ethiopian type [African] representation. I reflected that there had been Negroes in this country, and that this had been in the first epoch of the world."*

These heads are 8ft by 18ft in circumference and are made from a single piece of basalt rock. They date back to 800 - 600 B.C.E.

Although this was a major find and seventeen have been found all around the country; any publication asserting that these Colossal Heads were indeed images of Africans and built by Africans was at that time met with silence. It would be another 77 years in 1939, before National Geography Society researcher Matthew Stirling, with funding from the Smithsonian Institute, led an archaeological team to Tres Zapotes in Mexico and excavated the Colossal Head. It should also be noted that hundreds of images of Africans in terracotta, made between 1500 B.C.E. And 1500 C.E. have been found in the Americas. Many European scientists and scholars have tried to promote the notion that they are there because of Melanesian migration, but are opposed to the idea that Africans had made contact with the Americas millenniums ago.[4]

An interesting note for the reader is that the Nigerian city of Ile-Ife was paved in 1000 C.E. with decorations that originated in Ancient America. This took place 500 years before the time of Christopher Columbus is said to have discovered America. To understand how some European scholars underplay the African contribution please see what Dr Chancellor Williams has to say in Chapter 2 entitled Blatant Lies.

It must be noted as Africans travelled from one part of Africa to another and from Africa to the rest of the world, they were discovering how to make fire, the use of fire and inventing tools out of wood, bones and stone. Mining raw minerals from the earth and then smelting iron, inventing farming and farming equipment, language, animal husbandry, alphabets, writing and writing tools, paper from papyrus, calendars, medicines and civilized techniques for burying their dead etc.

With travelling, whether overland or across the waters, navigational skills would have been necessary and so it would have required knowledge in disciplines such as astronomy, physics, mathematics and geography. Also ship building and nautical know-how would have been employed as part of traversing the sea and oceans and, as evidenced, to other continents or land masses.

In the next few pages we explore just a few of the many inventions from Africa that shape what we all do today.

The African Origin of Technology

In an article written by Damien Gayle and published in the Daily Mail Newspaper, on 6th December 2012, entitled 'How Ancient Africans were the First Nerds' [and subtitled] 'Birth of technology traced back 70,000 years to the continent's [Africa] southern tip', Gayle writes that a new scientific paper claims how modern human

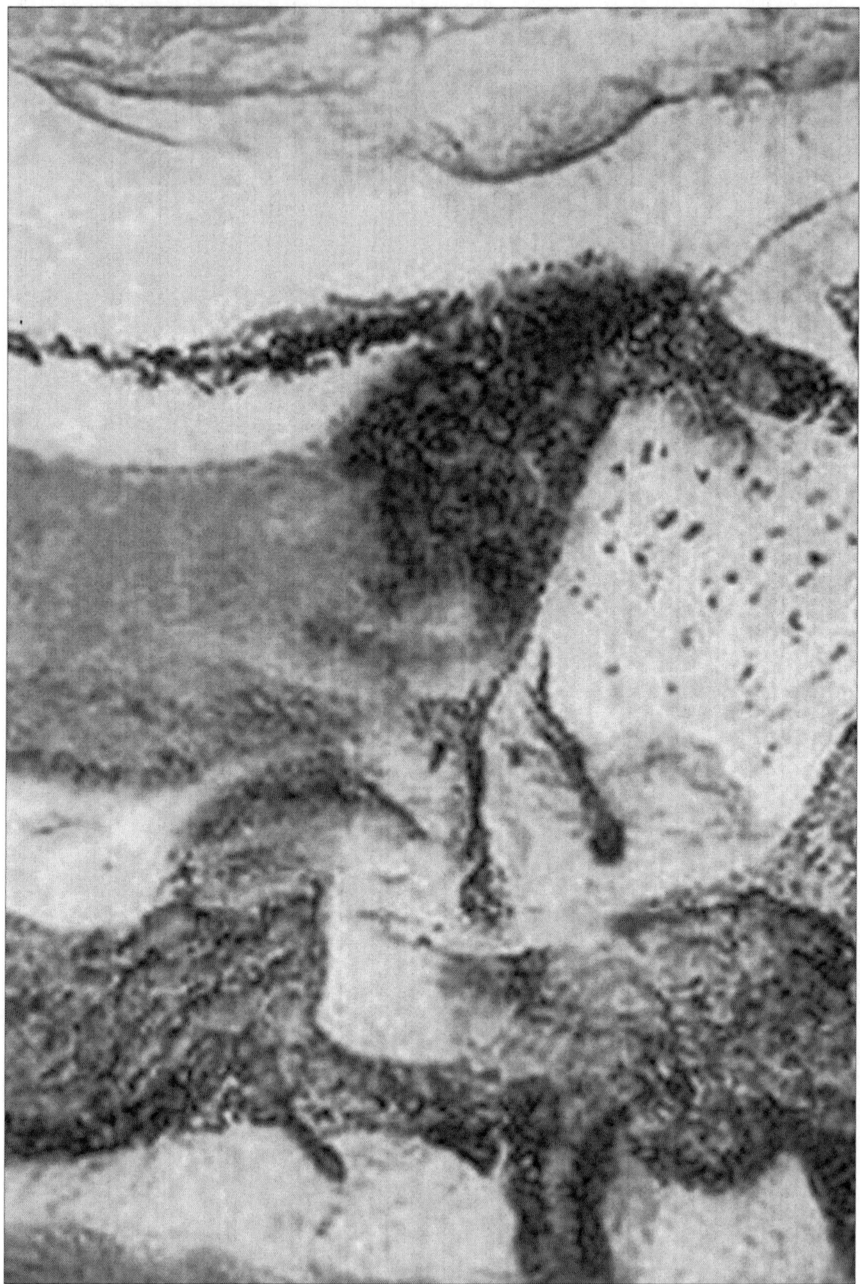

Gramaldi Mans Rock Art

Modern day Khoisan person

technology began more than 70,000 years ago in South Africa before spreading to communities elsewhere.[5]

Renowned archaeologist Professor Christopher Henshilwood of Wits University in South Africa, the author of the new scientific paper, says the most recent research decisively shows that Africa is the birthplace of modern human cognition.

The paper shows how the ancient Africans invented and innovated many things that modern man still uses today, such as the first abstract art (engraved ochre and engraved ostrich eggshell); the first jewellery (shell beads); the first bone tools; and the earliest use of the pressure flaking technique, that was used in combination with heating to make stone spear points and the first probable use of stone tipped arrows.

The findings in the paper highlight that:[6]

- Technology found in southern Africa predates similar artefacts found in Europe by 30,000 years
- Archaeologists claim it decisively shows that Africa is the birthplace of modern human cognition
- Findings debunk widely held belief that modern human behaviour originated in Europe 40,000 years ago.

Found at the Blombos Cave site, Southern Cape coastline, South Africa. c. 100,000

The African Origin of Farming and Animal Husbandry

Where would we be today without the skill of farming and the labour-saving devices we invented to make simpler the gruelling and back-breaking tasks that precede the sowing, planting and rearing in order to harvest, share and enjoy the produce at the end of it all?

Scientists and historians have failed to agree where in the world farming was invented. But if we work from the premise that Africans were the first people to inhabit the planet predicated on universally accepted archaeological findings, then Africans would have had to be either the first or amongst the first people to engage in farming. That said, agriculture appears to have been invented around 18,000 B.C.E. and evidence shows agricultural activity in Africa around that time.[7]

According to author Bayard Webster, in a paper entitled 'African Cattle Bones Stir Scientific Debate' published under the title, 'Blacks In Science', he says "A University of Massachusetts' anthropologist has found that the earliest known domestic cattle lived in East Africa (Kenyan Highlands) some 15,000 years ago." This would question many of the books which have stated that civilization started in the Middle East, where domesticated cattle were known to exist some 8000 years ago. Also, scientists have found that domesticated grain crops which date back to 18,000 years have been found in Africa. It can be seen that domesticated crops and cattle and the resulting equipment invented to rear them (fore runners of farming and animal husbandry) proves that African societies were more technologically advanced than given credit for by most European scholars.[8]

The Ploughshare, which is an integral part of farming again appears to have its origins in Africa. This invention then made its way throughout the world. From the land, Africans went on to animal husbandry, blacksmithing etc. Items from flora; such as plants, trees and herbs were turned into food and drink, medicines, clothing, adornment items, ink for writing, dyes for colouring clothing and painting etc. If we adopt the preceding premise, of Africa being the origins of man, then in order to proceed, we have to understand the world as it was then. Early man's existence 'back in the day' involved hunting and gathering for survival, which meant a nomadic life style, hence the migratory patterns as evidenced by all the anthropological studies done over the years on the continent. Temporary settlements were set up and dismantled as they moved on in their quest for more fertile pastures. Over time, however, there were certain places that they stayed longer than others, due to an abundance of nature's provisions.

This led to settlements that eventually turned into communities (common + unity). As these communities grew, subsistence farming developed as a temporary measure to support their stay; animal were reared (which later became husbandry) for use and consumption; security mechanisms were put in place against other hunters and gatherers, creating warriors to protect their community as they grew; and evidently more permanent structures – homes and homesteads- were built. As one can discern, these were the beginnings of 'a social, political and economic cultural set up that in turn bore civilizations such as Benin, Shonghai, Kemet, Nubia and Zimbabwe that went on to contribute massively to today's world.

The African Origin of Mining and Metals

It would appear that Africans have been mining minerals from around 45,000 B.C.E. In the Southern African landlocked country of Swaziland, a mine was discovered in the town of Ngwenya. The mine produced a mineral called Hamatite, which is a reddish iron oxide that can be used as a dye, ink or paint. The people used it for rock art (modern day writing and recording events).

There is evidence of wide usage of all major metals and alloys all over the continent. The Badri people of Egypt used copper as early as 4000 B.C.E. They made early types of chisels or axe-blade shape tools called celts. In Nubia, Bronze which is an alloy of tin and copper was being used around 3000 B.C.E. for making mirrors, daggers and vases. (Gibbs: 1995) In West Africa earliest recorded metal usage is copper appearing around the 1st millennium B.C.E.

Next to appear was iron mongering dating back to 1500 B.C.E. at Termit, Western Africa. Bronze appears around 1300 B.C.E. in the same region, all pre-dating the European and Asian import theory. This theory has been used to try to explain other similar world shattering discoveries, especially those that pre-date Europe's advent into Africa circa 15th century. The theory maintains that most of the so called signs of 'civilization' or 'civilized societies' exposed over the last couple of centuries, have been credited to excursions, incursions and 'visits' - by Asian travellers and even earlier claims of European travellers who imparted this knowledge to the African: but worse still, in their unwillingness to give any credit to the African creative mind they entertained the theory of Aliens/Martians from outer space having landed in Africa and brainwashed the earthlings, hence the presence of such advanced technologies and architectural designs on the continent!!

This thread of thought implies the lack of wherewithal or capability or even the mental fortitude of the African to have come up with such advanced developments. The various incredible developmental areas are touched upon herein at slightly greater depth than we are letting on.

When the British colonized Zimbabwe (formerly Great Zimbabwe) they said that Africans could not

Iron furnace found at Melville Koppies in South Africa, said to be bought by Bantu group of people into that region.

have built this great civilization. Historian Dr Y. Ben-Jochannan says that "they even went as far as saying that it was shipwrecked Greeks that built it, but when no evidence could be found, they looked further and said it was shipwrecked Chinese again no proof could be found and all evidence pointed to Africans." Under the leadership of Cecil Rhodes --- who renamed Zimbabwe, Rhodesia --- his government made it a crime, punishable by 6 months imprisonment, for Africans to teach that it was in fact their ancestors who built Great Zimbabwe. [9]

Some of the world's oldest structures and monuments can still be found in Africa. One only needs to travel to countries such as Egypt, Ethiopia, Kenya, Mali, Sudan, Tanzania and Zimbabwe, to see them. In the southern African countries of South Africa, Zimbabwe and Mozambique over 600 stone ruins have been found which date back to before 12th century C.E.. The Shona people of that region call these buildings Mazimbabwe, which means great revered houses of stone. The largest of these ruins is Great Zimbabwe, and is an area which consisted of 12 clusters of buildings spread over three miles enclosed in outer wall made of 10,000 tone granite rock in the 14th century C.E. The city housed over 18,000 residents.

In Egypt there are temples, structures and pyramids that date back as far as 5000 B.C.E. At this point it is important to note that Egypt is a country within the continent of Africa and not Asia or Europe. I only say this because many of us were taught in school that it was not in Africa even though the maps told us differently. Even as an adult whilst writing this book it seems as though the British Museum is still working along this ethos as they separate their Egyptian collection, which is on a prominent floor, from their African collection which is on a lower level (basement). Also while on that subject, when we are talking about pyramids, they can be the smooth sided pyramids or the step pyramids as in the case of the famous ones designed by the first engineer, the African multi-genius Imhotep in Sankara, circa 2630 B.C.E.. South of Egypt you will find Sudan and what many people do not know is that there are more pyramids in the Sudan than in Egypt; and guess what? There were pyramids also found in Ethiopia. The building of these great African monuments and in particular the pyramids, demonstrates that Africans were using complex mathematics which must have included a superior knowledge of Geometry, Trigonometry and Algebra etc. The same principles as the Pythagoras' Theorem must have been employed over 2000 years before he was born.

Please note that mathematician and historian Pythagoras travelled from Greece to Africa to receive a 22 year education in the African mystery systems that included maths and science. Many others such as French mathematician and physicist Baron Jean-Baptiste Joseph Fourier also studied Egyptian work whilst in Africa with Napoleon Bonaparte.

Along with the great building structures that can be found in Egypt, items that have also been found are things such as plates, cups, saucers and other pottery items. This demonstrates that African's were using the technology of pottery, which also involves the use of a kiln to fire the clay. Author Manyonyi Amalemba makes the point that "scientists, archaeologists and historians can't put a precise date on the invention of the Kiln but there's at least agreement that there is evidence linking pottery to the Bantu migratory period. It may be safe to make the assumption that the firing of kilns would date back to the same time period/era as that of the earliest recorded use of metals that is as early as the 1st millennia. The art of pottery making is still alive and well and they mostly use open fired kilns in sub-Saharan Africa (this art first evidenced around 3000 BCE.). They were there to serve specific and functional purposes - food preparation, water jars and most importantly alcohol storage. Relation to metal era is the use of forges and firing ovens for sculpture and moulds etc. as preceded herein..."

The Church of St. George is one of eleven rock-hewn churches of Lalibela, Ethiopia it is 25 meters wide and 30 meters high. This church and another ten churches are classified sites by UNESCO World Heritage Site under "Hewn Churches of Lalibela rock ." Lalibela is a pilgrimage site for members of the Ethiopian Orthodox Church, especially during the festival of Timqet.

Giza Necropolis

Pottery, Mangbetu - African objects in the American Museum of Natural History

Centres of Excellence

Africa can boast the world's oldest centres of learning; one only needs to look at ancient Egypt to find the oldest buildings of knowledge, which include temples and libraries. It was to ancient Egypt that both the Greek and Roman scholars went to receive an African education.

In West Africa during the Songhay Empire, Timbuktu was a world centre for trade and learning. The University of Djenne in Timbuktu - housed in three schools - would open its doors to all; even people from the Far East came to receive an African education. Other African centres of learning were Goa and Walata. Africans were not selfish with their knowledge they demonstrated this by building a university in Spain, the University of Salamanca, during their occupation and civilization of Southern Europe, circa 1134 C.E.

Great Mosque of Djenné, trio of minarets overlooks the central market of Djenné.

Personal Hygiene and Adornments

When we talk about personal hygiene and grooming, we don't have to leave Africa to find who the inventors of that were. An exhibition on African combs at both the Fitzwilliam Museum, Cambridge University and Bruce Castle Museum, Tottenham in 2013, showed quite clearly that the Afro-comb was invented in Africa and used by the ancient Egyptians for grooming, adornment and other symbolic reasons. Make-up and perfumes can also be found in this region and all over Africa. Both precious and non-precious metals and stones were also used by these ancient Africans for adornment purposes [accessorizing not preserve of modern society at all!!].

The African Origin of Electricity

In physics classes we are taught that electricity was discovered by scientists such as Benjamin Franklin in 1752 and the battery invented by Volta in 1800, but according to Nur Ankh Amen in his book 'The African Origins of Electromagnetism' there is evidence to show that the ancient Africans in Egypt had been able to invent a type of device that looks very much like the modern day battery and could produce electricity thousands of years before. The djed, which is the ancient Egyptian symbol for stability and is thought to represent the backbone of Osirus [Ausar], can be seen in the hieroglyphics on the temple walls. It is a pillar with bands across the top and base, and according to Nur Ankh Amen it is made by placing two dissimilar metals on either side of a papyrus soaked in salt water or acid, similar to how a modern day battery is made with copper, paper and zinc. [10]

The Written Word

Many people have been fooled into thinking Africa was not a literate culture and the only way they transferred stories and information was from memory - by word of mouth. This could not be further from the truth. Let me just say it is true that Africans did, and still do communicate stories verbally, as in the case of their Griots (aural social story- keepers/ tellers) which mostly are the fore runners of today's rappers, calypsonians, poets, message musicians etc. But they also wrote their stories and information down. Let me give a few examples in evidence of what I am saying. I'll start with the Khoi and San later renamed by Europeans as 'Grimaldi man' (who we spoke about earlier) and then later as 'Bushman'. From cave walls of South West Africa, all the way up to cave walls in Italy and the recent discoveries in Brazil, you can see the paintings or stories written by the Khoi and San people. These paintings date back to Circa 30,000 B.C.E. Think about it!

In an article reported in the New African magazine, dated September 2011, Christopher Ehert, a leading Professor of African historical linguistics at the University of California, said,

> "Long before the emergence of Egyptian hieroglyphs, Africa had a wealth and diversity of graphic and plastic symbols that recorded and communicated information, without being systematically related to language... systems such as - knotted cords, tallies, rock art, pottery design, etc. – were precursors to writing and are often referred to as 'proto-writing.' These systems are among those that might have provided graphic inspiration for Egyptian hieroglyphs."

Now to Egypt, let's look at tools for inscribing words and images. We can find some of the earliest forms or tools for scribing/writing in Egypt and we can see what they 'scribed/wrote', by looking inside their temples. These Africans also invented a type of paper which was made from the 'Papyrus' plant, that grows along the Nile river (the word 'paper' believed to be a derivative). On this paper they would write in their language which the Greeks later called hieroglyphic script, but the ancient Egyptians, called Medu-Neter, which demonstrates how sacred writing was to them as Medu-Neter means "divine speech, tongue of God or the word of God".

As well as the Medu Neter script, Africans have invented many other scripts which include gicandi symbols used by the Kikuyu in Kenya, adinkra used in Ghana and Cote d'Ivoire, nsibidi symbols among the Igbo, Ibibio, and Ejagham in Nigeria and the cosmographic systems employed among the Dogon in Mali and Kongo used in Angola.[11] Other languages invented in Africa were the Phoenician script, Tifinagh script which is a descendent of Phoenician script. In eastern Africa, other written scripts were invented which include; Ge'ez and Amharic, around the 10th Century C.E. It was mainly used by the Ethiopian Coptic church. In northern Africa the Nubians had invented the Merioitic Kushite script between 2nd and 3rd century B.C.E. Later on they also created Old Nubian scripts which date back to about 10th century C.E.

In the 1800s two new scripts were created in West Africa. They were the Vai script, which may have been influenced by Cherokee syllabary, due to it being brought by North American missionaries into Liberia, but Prince Momulu Massa quoi III, educator and author, in papers on Via script, says it has its origins in the Nile valley.[12] The other is the Bamum script, which is indigenous to the Cameroon and was created around 1896 C.E. It should also be noted that the Bamum script is a number writing-system. [13]

I think we can conclude that the blatant misconception created by 18th to 20th century European scientists and scholars that Africa was a non-literate culture and had no form of written or recording script has now been exposed as nonsense. It can be seen in this article that from the earliest time of human civilization Africans were the inventors of writing, and this can be seen in African Rock Art by the San and Khoi people and also in the creation of the (ancient) Egyptian Medu Neter (5,000 B.C.E.), to the Phoenician scripts, culminating with the more recent West African Bamum script. At St. John's University in New York, professor Dr. Konrad Tuchscherer believes that European script, and in fact most scripts around the world, except for the Chinese script, can find origins in the Africa script and in particular the Medu Neter script.[14]

Medu Neter script

Adinkra symbols, each symbol has a meaning.

Time and Seasons

The first solar calendar in Egypt appears to be around 11,652 B.C. According to author C.R. Gibbs, in Kenya, the site at Namoratunga II was used for astronomical reasons. The stone pillars there were aligned to various stars or constellations including Sirius, Aldebraran, the Pleiades, and central Orion. He goes on to say that an article in the Science magazine (May 19, 1978), states that the astronomical sites in Kenya provide insight into the scientific contribution of early African people, an aspect of black studies often ignored by historians.[15] In the West African country of Mali, in 1935, a 25 year study was carried out by French scientists, Marcel Griaule and Germaine Dieterlen on the Dogon people. The study found that the Dogon had superior astronomical knowledge. They had already observed four of Jupiter's moons, several spiral galaxies, the Sirius star cluster and the rings of Saturn way before Europeans and without a telescope. The study in full can be found in the book 'The Pale Fox.'

The African Origin of Mathematics

The earliest artefact showing mathematical knowledge of Africans was that of a Baboon's fibula bone found by the Lebombo mountain region in Swaziland, which dates back to 35,000 years. The bone was used as a measuring instrument. The earliest artefact which illustrates the advance mathematical knowledge of Africans was discovered by leading Belgium archaeologists in the 1950s on the border of the Rwanda and the Democratic Republic of Congo, at the Ishango fishing site next to Lake Edward, originally called Rutanzige. Dr Claudia Zaslavsky the author of 'Africa Counts' says that from a mathematical point of view the most interesting find is a small bone-tool discovered there. It is a piece of animal bone about 10cm long, having notches arranged in definite patterns within three distinct columns and a bit of quartz fixed in a narrow cavity in its head. Belgium archaeologist Ann Hauzeur says

> "What sets this bone apart from the other fossils found at Ishango is the markings on the bone; they are very well organised, they are not made at random".

The markings suggest that they follow a number system based on ten, twelve, a knowledge of multiplication and prime numbers. Brussels Bureau Chief, Patricia Kelly says that:

> "The Quartz at the tip of the bone may have been used for writing or engraving."

The bone could also possibly be a forerunner to the modern pen. The Ishango bone was first believed to date back to 9000 B.C.E., but more recent and advanced scientific research on the bone tool dates it back to over 20,000 years. Kelly goes on to say

> "The Ishango Bone proves that there was a highly advanced civilization that existed in central Africa 15,000 years before Pharonic Egyptian culture, therefore Homo sapiens may have evolved in central Africa before anywhere else in the world."

Mathematician Dr Dirk Huylebrouck of the Belgium Museum says,

> "We now have more proof of mathematical activity in Africa,

> which can be found on bones, stones and strings. There is good reason to believe that it's the first mathematical activity...it's my opinion that it should be placed on a golden table at the entrance to the museum."

Some scientists believe that Ishango man's number system travelled north as far as Egypt and west as far as western Africa.

In the 1850s, a German, Henry Rhind, found a papyrus which had recordings left by Ah'mose, scribe, senmut [architect and government official] and adviser to Queen Hatshepsut. This papyrus dates back to over 3500 years. Ah'mose's papyrus which was later named the Rhind papyrus tells us a lot about Egyptian mathematics. Within the text it contains 85 problems of a practical nature, the use of fractions, and the solution of equations. Another one of the great African mathematicians and scientists was the brilliant Hypatia, who lived around 370 B.C.E., the daughter of mathematician Theon. Hypatia lectured on mathematics, philosophy, physics and astronomy. She wrote important and complex mathematical papers. She also invented an apparatus for distilling water. Even thousands of years before both Ah'mose and Hypatia, lived Imhotep, a mathematician, the real father of medicine and the world's first multi-genius. Imhotep was the architect who designed the stepped pyramid at Saqqara, which we can still see today in Egypt after over 5000 years later.

I have only scratched the surface of the African contributions to mathematics within this publication. For further research read the works of Claudia Zaslavsky,

Beatrice Lumpkin, Ron Eglash, Cheikh Anta Diop and Ivan Van Sertima.

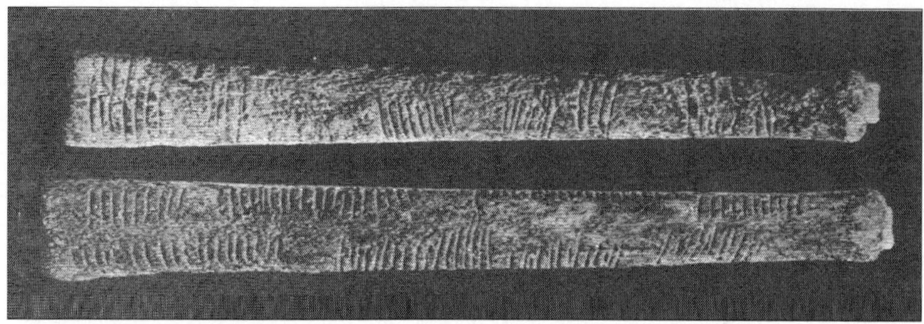

The Ishango bone is a bone tool, dated to the Upper Paleolithic era.

Notes & References:

1. A Guide To East Africa, Eyewitness Travel Kenya, P. Briggs & L. Williams, Dorlington Kingsley, 2009. | 2. Ibid | 3. Discoveries Challenge Beliefs on Humans' Arrival in the Americas, Simon Romero,The New York times , March 27, 2014. | 4 New African Mag, Miriam Jimenez Roman, Tom Mbakwe, pg 15-18. | 5. How Ancient Africans were the First Nerds, Damien Gayle The Daily Mail, 6 December 2012. | 6. Ibid. | 7. Blacks In Sciences, pg 58. | 8. Ibid pp 65-66. | 9. Our Story, Dr. Yosef ben-Jochannan. | 10. The African Origins Of Electromagnetism, pg. | 11. Curtis Abraham, New African Magazine, Aug/Sept 2011 pg 83. | 12. C. R.Gibbs, Black Inventors, Pg 35. | 13. Curtis Abraham, New African Magazine, Aug/Sept 2011 pg 87. | 14. Ibid pp 84. | 15. C. R.Gibbs, Black Inventors, pg 44.

Web References:

www.youtube.com/watch?v=VX90IN8VSME&feature=youtube_gdata_player | www.youtube.com/watch?v=LXRvwk12atw | Dr Ron Eglash | Black Women Scientists & Inventors Vol 1, M. Williams, Djehuti-Ankh-Kheru | http://www.math.buffalo.edu/mad/Ancient-Africa/ishango.html | http://www.math.buffalo.edu/mad/Ancient-Africa/lebombo.html | http://realhistoryww.com/world_history/ancient/Misc/Prehistoric_Art/Grimaldi.htm | http://uk.aska.com/question/where-was-paper-invented | http://muse.jhu.edu/journals/hia/summary/v032/32.1alpern.htm

Time Line 1 - Early History

Time Line 1
Early History

- **6 Million** years ago ape-like man or Hominid's, called Orrorin Tugenensis, lived in Africa.

- **3.9 million** years ago lived another type of Hominid they called him Australopithecus Africanus.

- **2.8 million** years - Lucy - Bones found in Ethiopia

- **1.9 million** years old bones discovered at Olduvai/Oldupai (maasai for wild sisal plant) Gorge Tanzania. (1953 Dr. Leaky) They gave him the name Zinjanthropus that translates to south - eastern Africa man.

- **1.8 Million** Homo erectus

- **250,000 B.C.E.** Homo-sapiens or Modern man

- **40, 000 B.C.E.** Modern man travels from Africa to Europe

- **35,000 B.C.E.** Lebombo Bone found in Lebombo mountains between south Africa and Swaziland (Used for mathematics calculations and a moon/lunar cycles, probably early,calendar)

- **30,000 B.C.E.** Iron Smelting takes place in Southern Africa.

- **30,000 B.C.E.** Britain emerges from its last Ice age.

- **20,000 B.C.E.** Ishango Bone used for mathematical calculations (Congo/Rwanda region).

- **28,000 B.C.E.** Writing Systems in Africa (Petroglyps and Prototypes)

- **18,000 B.C.E.** Farming in east Africa.

- **15,000 B.C.E.** Animal Husbandry takes place in Kenya

- **12,000 B.C.E.** Grimaldi Man (Africans) arrive in Europe
- **11,652 B.C.E.** The first solar calendar in Egypt
- **10,000 B.C.E.** The first Lunar calendar in Egypt
- **8,000 B.C.E.** Pottery takes place in Kenya and the Congo
- **8,000 B.C.E.** Iberian Celts (Africans) enter Briton
- **7,000-5000 B.C.E.** Briton-Celts (white) enter Briton from France & Germany.
- **3,500 B.C.E.** Ah'mose Papyrus (Rhind Papyrus) - [paper derivative name later]
- **3,000 B.C.E.** Building of Stonehenge in England
- **2,630 B.C.E.** (Imhotep) The Step Pyramids in Egypt
- **1,500 B.C.E.** some Celti-Iberian return back to Africa from Europe because of violent encounters with Nordics and Scythians
- **5th century B.C.E. - 8th cent B.C.E.** Paper (Papyrus)

Other great African Civilizations from the 6th to 1th Century B.C.E.

- **6th millennium - 3rd century B.C.E.** Sumeria
- **4th millennium - 6th century B.C.E.** Elam
- **4th millennium B.C.E. onwards** Kush
- **4th millennium B.C.E. - 1000 C.E.** Nok
- **3rd millennium - 5th century B.C.E.** Indus Valley

- **2nd millennium B.C.E. - 7th century C.E.** Arabia Felix
- **2nd millennium B.C.E. - 10th century C.E.** Ethiopia
- **7th - 2nd century B.C.E. -** Carthage
- **3rd - 1st century B.C.E.** Numidia
- **370 B.C.E.** Hypatia (Scientists, Mathematician and Inventor) daughter of Scientists, Theon
- **1391-1271 B.C.E. - rabbinical dates** - (D.O.B. alternatives 1592 -jerome/1619- Uusher) Birth of the Biblical Moses disputed [He was mistaken for Pharaohs Son, so he must have had to look like that African King] - was adopted by pharaohs daughter and brought up by her after the discovery in reeds as a baby) mixed race Jewish and Egyptian (Hebrew/Canaanite)
- **7-2 BCE. to 30 - 33 C.E.** Birth of the Historical Jesus (skin like amber, feet like fine brass burnt in an oven (black) and hair like wool)) Revelations 1:12-18.
- **43 B.C.E.** - Romans enter Briton again led by Emperor Claudius he is met with fierce resistance from the Black Silures who live in Briton.
- **55 B.C.E. -** Romans enter Briton led by General (Emperor) Julius Caesar.
- **79 C.E. -** Britian becomes a province of Rome.
- **146 C.E. -** Emperor Septimius Severus is born in Africa, This African later becomes emperor of the Roman Empire.
- **176 C.E. -** Emperor Septimius Severus (The African) rules Britain (he also supervises the restoration of Hadrian's Wall).

Part III: Chapter 4 -

Evidence of Early Black Presence in the British Isles

CHAPTER 4

Evidence of Early Black Presence in the British Isles

Blacks occupied the British Isles from approximately 8,000 B.C.E. and for at least 7,000 years before various Germanic tribes and others entered Britain. This may sound like nonsense to some, simply because most have not been taught this in school, nevertheless it does not make it any less true. Peoples such as the Caribs, Arawak, Siboney and Taino, sometimes mistakenly referred to as Red Indians, at one time occupied the Caribbean. If we look in most Caribbean countries today we would be hard pushed to find any. They are practically extinct, mainly because of European forced occupation, slavery and diseases they caught from their occupiers which they had no defence against.

Just 500 years ago, according University of the West Indies' professor [Sir] Hilary Beckles, there were over 8 million of them in the Caribbean - they were the majority people. So if that could have happened to a people in just 5 hundred years, it should not seem a fantasy that black people once occupied the British Isles in large numbers thousands of years ago. Moreover in Kwame Osei's book 'The Ancient Egyptian Origins of the English Language', he writes that Roman historian Pliny saw the ancient Britons in the second century C.E. and he describes some of them of having complexion as dark as Ethiopians.

Africans in Early Europe

The true history of Britain in my opinion is one that has never been taught. When children are presented with so called British history at school it usually starts around the year 1066 and what happened after that. Some might go a little further back and start after 3rd century C.E., and if you're lucky you may be taught a little about Roman Britain, but very little to no information on what took place before then.

In most European books the Phoenicians often appear to be a mysterious people, never clear on their ethnicity or heritage. This is further confused by the way they have been depicted on television. The Phoenicians, who were great seafarers, had navigated from North Africa and visited much of Europe, and North America where they even established a settlement in Florida. They were sent to the West on the bidding of their African Israelite leader King Solomon. During this period the seal of Solomon was carved on stones throughout Scotland (A. Muhammad, Pg 41: 2004). From the above paragraph it can be seen quite clearly that these mysterious people - the Phoenicians from North Africa - were of African stock.

Earlier we spoke about Grimaldi Man, the man from Africa who travelled throughout the world with the emblem of fire and the dragon, and left traces wherever he travelled, such as paintings on cave walls in Europe. Later Grimaldi was succeeded in Europe by another type of African who was physically shorter in appearance, lived mainly in Spain and was called Iberian by the Greeks. He also became known as the Iberian-Celt.[1] Approximately 8000-3000 B.C.E. he spread throughout Europe, as far east as Russia and Northwest to Britain. There is plenty of evidence to back this up, but let me present here just one piece. According to David W. Koeller, 'the Venus of Willendorf' is the name that was given to a female figurine that was found in 1908 by an archaeologist named Joseph Szombathy at a paleolithic site near the town of Willendorf in Austria. It is now in the Natural Historisches Museum in Vienna. The statue was carved from oolitic limestone and was coloured with red ochre. It measures 110mm in height and is dated approximately between 30,000 and 25,000 B.C.E.[2] The Venus figurine is shaped like some women from southern Africa, (the most famous being Sarah 'Saartjie' Baartman) who are shaped with more steatopygia than average women. European explorers first called them Hottentot (now an offensive term); they were named so by the Dutch settlers in imitation of the sound of their language. Incidentally, I have recently discovered that these types of figurines were also found across the island of Malta and can be seen in the Valletta Museum.

These people were the ancients of Europe and indeed the British Isles. With them they brought their culture and part of their culture was the introduction of new sciences, technologies and inventions. One of the most important was the Ploughshare which they called the Heiralpha and translates to Heiral – 'Holy' and Pha – 'one'. These black people, similar to their brothers in Africa, revered the land and so called their invention which tills the land - holy. They also brought to Britain agricultural science and other tools, pottery making and technologies for mining iron, copper, silver and salt which Africans were already doing in African countries and Empires such as Sudan, Egypt, Ethiopia, Songhay, Benin, Ghana etc.[3]

The First Scientific Wonder in Britain

For centuries many English scientists and historians have wondered why and how Stonehenge was built. The relics of this magnificent structure can still be seen today in Wiltshire, southern England and continues t attract millions of tourists. Stonehenge, which according to historian Gerald Massy means 'hung up', is a stone structure built in a circular fashion and scientists have dated its origins to about 4000 years B.C.E. - by far the oldest remaining stone structure in the British Isles.

Let me be controversial for a moment. One thing which I have noticed when studying ancient relics such as the pyramids in Egypt, Africa, ancient temples of Malta, the ancient structures in Great Zimbabwe, the African statues in Easter Islands or the Olmec Heads in Mexico, if western Europeans were not involved in their construction and instead all the logical evidence points to the African mind creating them, often times western scholars will try and give the credit to anyone else rather than the African. They have even gone as far as saying some paranormal forces built them. They have said Great Zimbabwe was built by the Chinese, even though the Chinese have refuted those claims. They have also said the pyramids of Egypt were built by aliens. Let me add for your reference that there are more pyramids in Sudan than Egypt and some have been found even as far as Ethiopia. All that said, if Africans were to say that they were the original builders of Britain's most ancient monument most people would laugh and many a historian would deny this and prefer to say we y have no idea who built it and how it got there.

Let's look at what three brave British archaeologist and historians have to say about the inventors and builders of Stonehenge. Gerald Massy, Godfrey Higgins and David Mac Ritchie, have said that Stonehenge was designed and built by a black race of people. Massay says a Negro architect called Morien, who most likely came from Egypt designed and built them. Higgins believes that it was built by the ancient Buddhas of India- these ancient Buddhas were all woolly-haired, flat-nosed and thick lipped people. He says,

"A great nation called the Celtae, of whom the Druids were the priest..."[4]

David MacRitchi e cites a writer in his book 'Ancient and Modern Britons':

> "...in so far as I have been able to observe, the black race is superior to the fair in stature and strength... in respect to intellect, they are acute, accurate observers of natural phenomena, quick of apprehension and fluent in speech. In their moral character they are at least much superior to the population of most of the low land parishes."[5]

US President Barack Obama visited the historical site of Stonehenge in Amesbury, Wiltshire, England touring the prehistoric monument. September 2014

The African Roman Emperor in England

It's believed that the Romans first came to the British Isles in 55 B.C.E., on an expedition led by Emperor Julius Caesar, who was then a general. They then came back and conquered Britain around 49 – 79 C.E., led by Emperor Claudius. This took him over 30 years to achieve because his Roman army met strong resistance from the Silures (a black tribe) who occupied the land alongside fragmented white tribes. The Romans would go on to occupy the lands of Britain or as they named it Britannia, for up to 330 years.[6] During the Roman occupation of Britain, the lands passed through the control of several Roman emperors and officials, and some of these emperors and officials were Africans. When we are taught about the conquest of Britain in school history lessons many of us can score an 'A' grade without mentioning anything about the African involvement, simply because this part of the Roman conquest is not taught. In the book 'A History of Black People in London', the author states in the opening sentence that

> "There have been black people [living] in Britain since Roman times, when an African division of Roman soldiers was stationed near Carlisle, defending Hadrian's Wall in the third century [C.E.]."

Romans were known for assimilating the people they conquered into their armies in order to expand their empire. Some of those conquered were Africans, who eventually ascended to the very top ranks of the Roman army as well as society.

The Roman Emperor Septimius Severus, an African, conquered Britain In 208 C.E. Emperor Septimius Severus was born on 11th April 146 C.E. His land of birth was Libya in North Africa, he was born to an upper middle class African family. During his childhood he was taught Latin, jurisprudence, military science and astrology. Severus entered the Roman Senate around 173 C.E. and in 193 C.E. was declared the Roman Emperor.

In 208 C.E. he led troops to Britain in order to quash rebellions from the Pics and Celts from the North and to restore and upgrade Hadrian's Wall. Most of his top officials were Africans, and he was so connected to his African roots that his eating habits had not changed; he would order his troops only to get food from Africa for him. Incidentally there is evidence that Septimius Severus travelled to Egypt in 202 C.E. where it is believed he researched and studied the ancient African Mystery systems. Septimius Severus died in York of pneumonia in 211 C.E.[7]

What Did the Romans Contribute to the Development of Britain?

Let us not forget what the Romans gave to Britain, for example: road infrastructure, defence systems such as Hadrian's Wall, the calendar, central heating, aqueducts (water bridges), an early pumping/sewage system, indoor plumbing, heated baths, towns, public libraries, firemen, paved streets, cement, bricks, language (i.e. Latin), notwithstanding a century of peace, and this is just to name a few. At this point it should be noted that in terms of knowledge, philosophy, science, mathematics and technology etc. Rome was the daughter of Greece and the grand-daughter of Egypt, Africa.

Moorish Science in Europe

In 7 C.E. a group of African people leave North Africa for Europe by way of Spain, settling in a region which became known as Gibraltar. It derives its name from the leader of the people who travelled to that region, his name was Gebel Tarik and his people became known as Moors. It must be noted at the time when the Moors entered Europe, the Romans had long gone and the civilization and science that they brought had either been forgotten or not built upon. These were Europe's dark ages and in Britain they were experiencing constant invasions from savage tribes from places such as Germany, Denmark and Norway. But it would be the Moors who would light up Britain once more with their knowledge of science and mathematics. The Moorish scholars brought with them the Arabic numeral system, which included the zero, they also brought knowledge of chemistry, medicine, physics and astronomy.[8]

The Black Scottish King

Forest Whitaker was not the last black King of Scotland, oh no! Historian, MacRitchie mentions the dominance of Moors and their kings in Scotland before and after the Saxon kings of England. Up until the tenth century three provinces in Scotland were entirely black and the supreme ruler of these became, for a time, the paramount king of Transmaarine Scotland.

One of these kings was the King of Alban (Scotland), known in the history books as Kenneth, sometimes called Dubh or Niger.[9] At that time Scotland was split into several divisions and he ruled over three of the seven divisions. King Kenneth was constantly at war with the surrounding white divisions and finally the leader Fionn - 'the White' defeated him and drove the black king out for at least 20 years. But a son of King Kenneth called Kenneth Mac Dubh regained kingship for his father in 997 C.E. and reigned until 1004 C.E.[10]

Let's take a closer look at his bloodline. On the website Africa Resources, the author states:

> "...Kenneth III was King of Scotland from 997 to 1005 C.E. He was the son of King Dubh (Dub mac Mail Choluim – 962-967 C.E.), fourth cousin of the previous king Constantine III, and first cousin of his successor Malcolm II. Kenneth was the last King of Scotland [and not Forest Whitaker or Idi Amin, emphasis mine] to succeed to the throne through the tanistry system (passing on titles and lands), whereby the succession was shared between two family lines, and the dying king named his successor from the other family line.
>
> This system led to constant struggle between the ruling

families and was abandoned. Kenneth and his son Giric were both killed at Monzievaird, Tayside in 1005 CE. His first cousin Malcolm succeeded him and abolished the tanistry system by killing all of his male descendants. However Kenneth had a granddaughter, Gruoch, via his daughter Boite, whose first husband was Gillacomgain. They had a son called Lulach. She then married King Macbeth I of Scotland (becoming Lady Macbeth).

On the death of Macbeth her son via her first marriage, Kenneth III's great grandson, succeeded to the throne, to become King Lulach of Scotland. According to this history, the blood of Kenneth flows through the royal houses of Scotland. This story captures a curious fact about the Gaels from Gallicia – some were dark and have left many traces in Irish, Welsh and Scots clans..."

The Black Tudors of England During the 1500s

According to the book 'A History of Black Presence in London', during Tudor England all black people were referred to as Moors or Negros, which later developed into Blackamoors and Blackmoores. There is evidence of these black people living in Tudor England not only enslaved but also as free-living people, trading and working. This evidence can be found in historical records and paintings. One such recording is that of John Blanke, a musician [a trumpeter] who in 1507 was employed by the courts of Henry VII and later Henry VIII. He was paid 20s a month. [11]

John Blanke, Trumpeter

The Black Poor of London are Expelled to Sierra Leone

During the American War of Independence of 1775 - 1783 both the rebels/patriots and the loyalists (loyal to Britain) asked for the help of enslaved Africans. In the case of the British Loyalists they were able to convince over 1,500 black men to fight alongside them and in return they were promised their freedom. After the war the promise was kept and some went and settled in Nova Scotia in Canada, but the vast majority came to England and settled mainly in London. Whilst in London most could not get jobs or housing, while the white loyalists that had fought alongside the black loyalists, received a pension for their war efforts. Most of the black loyalist did not receive a pension from the British government and by 1784, there were over a thousand penniless and homeless black people walking the streets of London. The black poor also included Indians from India (Lascars) who were employed on British ships, but their employers often refused to pay them any money.[12]

The Committee of Relief for the Black Poor

In the late 18th Century a 'Committee of Gentlemen' was set up with the objective to seek relief for the Lascars, and soon extended its activities to help other black people in need. (Fryer: 1984) In 1786 the 'Committee for the Relief of the Black Poor' was set up to help raise money from the public in order to provide the black poor with broth, a piece of bread and meat.[13]. The aid effort had cost an estimated £20,000, but only £890 came from private funds, the rest had been paid for by the government.[14] They also gave money to the black poor, but there were strings attached, because the government wanted them off the streets of London and out of the country. They had to sign contracts saying in order to receive this relief they would be sent to Sierra Leone. This was problematic for the government as many of them did not want to go to Sierra Leone or anywhere along the West African coast, as they knew that Africans were still being kidnapped, taken to the Americas and forced into slavery.

Send Them Back

In order to get around this problem the British Government sought the services of a black leader of that time, Olaudah Equiano. At first Equiano tried to help but when he pointed out all the Government's flaws, in particular his complaints about the corruption and mistreatment of the black poor by Joseph Irwin, he was swiftly sacked.

Author and African abolitionist Ottobah Cugoano who was openly against the forced repatriation said

> "For can it be readily conceived that government would establish a free colony for them nearly to the spot, while it supports its forts and garrisons, to ensure, merchandise, and carry others into captivity and slavery?"[15]

The deportation continued without the help of Equiano. But what fate awaited the deported Africans of London? When the expedition left England in April 1787 and arrived in Sierra Leone the following month, it was just in time for the rainy season. The disaster that many feared ensued, of the four hundred people who sailed away from England, fifty died at sea, fifty-two more within a month of arrival. The locals destroyed a settlement in Granville Town. It was a major struggle for survival for the deportees. After just 4 years, only 60 of the 400 were still alive.[16]

A Word on Equiano – the African

Below is an excerpt written by historian Des Robinson and Michael Williams first published in the BIS Publications' Freedom Fighters Pack.

Olaudah Equiano was born in 1745 in the Biafra, Nigeria, he was part of the Igbo nation. As a child he was kidnapped and enslaved, taken to Barbados, eventually finding his way to England as a slave for a Royal Navy captain. Through his own determination and persistence which included his ability to buy and sell goods to sailors, planters, enslaved Africans and others during his travels all around the Caribbean, he was able to buy himself out of his enslavement. As a free person he continued a sailor's life which took him all around the world. He also learnt the science of Desalination whilst working as an assistant to Dr Irving. Equiano also dedicated his life to the complete abolition of the evil trade in humans which he had experienced first-hand.

In 1789, Equiano published "The Interesting Narrative of the Life of Olaudah Equiano", which became an almost instant best seller. As an anti-slavery work it was exceptional. It charted the terrifying experiences he had since he was a child, in a vivid manner. This exposed, in no uncertain terms, the holocaust that Africans were facing so that planters in the "New World" could obtain labour to enrich themselves and their motherland.

The intelligent Equiano dispelled the prevalent racist myth of the inferiority of the African and was read widely by the aristocracy. He married an English woman named Susanna Cullen, who bore him two children. He became a very wealthy man of almost celebrity status, with an estate that today would be worth over £100,000 (in 2015 that would be equivalent to approximately one million pounds). Unfortunately Equiano did not see the day he had been working relentlessly for, as he died on 31st March 1797, thirty-seven years before the official British abolition of slavery.

However, as an abolitionist Olaudah Equiano was a remarkable man of high moral fibre who never gave up on his principles.

Olaudah Equiano, known in his lifetime as Gustavus Vassa, was a prominent African in London, a freed enslaved person who was fundamental to the British movement to end the Trans-Atlantic slave trade.

Notes & References:
1. A frican People European Holidays II, Pg 10. | 2. [http://www.thenagain.info/webchron/world/Willendorf.html] | 3. African People European Holidays Vol II, Ishakamusa Barashango, 1983). pg 10. | 4. Sex & Race Vol 1, pg 197. | 5. Ancient and Modern Britons | 6. Afrikan People European Holidays Vol II, pg 35. | 7. Ibid pp 39. | 8. Ibid pp47. | 9. Ibid | 10. Ibid | 11. History or Black presence in London, pg 6. | 12. Ibid pp 22. | 13. Ibid pp | 14. The Trader, The Owner, The Slave, Walvin pg 245. | 15. Ibid pp 246. | 16. Ibid pp 247.

Web References:
http://www.raceandhistory.com/cgibin/forum/webbbs_config.plmd=read;id=2225 | http://www.raceandhistory.com/cgi-bin/forum/webbbs_config.pl?md=read;id=2225 | Free Your Mind, A. Muhammad pg 15. Ancient & Modern Britons, David Mac Ritchie. | http://www.africaresource.com/rasta/sesostris-the-great-the-egyptian-hercules/the-african-kings-of-scotland-the-black-celtish-clans-1/Sex and Race, Vol 1, JA. Rogers | http://www.nationalarchives.gov.uk/pathways/blackhistory/work_community/poor.htm | The History of Black Presence In London, GLC. | Africa's Gift to Europe: What You Were Never Taught In History Lessons 2003 Calendar, | BIS Publications, Michael Williams. | The Fight For Freedom Pack. D. Robinson, C. Soso, M. Williams, BIS Publications, 2007.

Part IV: Chapter 5 -

The Trans-Atlantic Enslavement Trade

"A people without knowledge of their [true] past history, origin and culture is like a tree without roots."
The Most Honourable Marcus Mosiah Garvey.

CHAPTER 5

The Trans-Atlantic Enslavement Trade

"Christopher Columbus that Damn Blasted Liar" **- Culture.**

Historians say that an Italian / Spanish sailor called Christopher (Colon) Columbus discovered America in 1492. In his attempt to sail to India he took a wrong turn and ended up in the Americas. Although he found people already occupied the Caribbean islands and the Americas, his-story records that Columbus discovered that area and much of that entire area was then renamed including the native people. It should also be noted according to author Rev. Barashango that on his way to the Caribbean both Columbus[1] and a fellow Italian pirate Amerigo Vespucci find Africans sailing back from the Americas to Africa. The native people of America explain to the European explorers that we have been trading with the Africans for years. This is the side of history, which is not taught in schools. In 1507 the landmass we now call

America is given that name by German cartographer Martin Waldseemuller, in honour of cartographer, sailor and financier Amerigo Vespucci who sailed there in March 9th 1454.[2]

What happened to the native people that Christopher Columbus claimed to have discovered in the Americas and Caribbean? Both authors have found that in most of the information available on this subject, there are no definitive statistics of how many indigenous peoples of the Caribbean were in the region at the time. The only indications are that there were populations that extended over most of the islands having migrated from the South American mainland and some from the north.

In the book "The Nonsense Guide to World History", author Chris Brazier writes that the impact of the Spanish on the Native people of Latin America is one of the most terrifying episodes in human history. In 1565 there were 21 million Indians in Mexico and less than 100 years later in 1607 there were just 1 million left, this story is similar all over the Americas and the Caribbean. The native peoples who lived for thousands of years in those lands within a very short time of European arrival, died from diseases caught from their new occupiers. Many also died from the enforced labour of working the gold and silver mines that were the driving motive of the Spanish colonization making Spain very wealthy.

It's important that this historical information is known for a number of reasons; for example the few native-Americans that still exist in that region are often portrayed as the immigrants in a similar way to the aboriginal people of Australia and New Zealand. With the genocide of the native people, other people would have to be enslaved to continue the growth of Spanish wealth and this shows just how Spain and other western European countries really got very wealthy so quickly.

The Transatlantic Enslavement Trade (15th Century - 20th Century)

This took place between 15th to the 19th century, in total up to 500 years. Britain's involvement was about 200 Years. What type of slavery was used during the trans-Atlantic Enslavement of Africans? It was Chattel Slavery, the worst type of slavery ever to be forced on another member of the human family. Chattel Slavery is where the enslaved African becomes no more than property, his or her destiny is totally in the hands of their European enslaver.

John Hawkins & His Cousin Sir Francis Drake...Heroes or Crooks?

It all depends on what position you take regarding the enslavement of one human being by another. Let's just take a moment to exam these two men and their relationship with the Triangular Enslavement Trade.

Admiral Sir John Hawkins, to give him his right title, was a leading mariner and Naval Administrator during the reign of Queen Elizabeth I. He is famous and is featured highly within the historical annals of England and Spain (in part).

Hawkins is known for the introduction of various new produce and artefacts, brought from his voyages, into the English culture; potatoes, tobacco and even sited as having brought the word shark into the English vocabulary (believed to have originated from the Mayan word for fish - Xoc). He was Knighted by the Queen for his contributions and services, in the defeat of the Spanish Armada in 1588.

Hawkins was born 1532 in Plymouth, Devon, into a wealthy seafaring family. His father, William Hawkins, was the Mayor and then MP (member of parliament), of Plymouth Town and was one the first to visit Guinea on the west coast of Africa, earlier in the 16th century. He was a privateer, a title that had been given to those that pirated treasure from attacking and robbing returning Spanish galleons, of their treasures, in the English channel, as they returned from voyages.

These privateers were known and often times, licensed by the royals and other business interests, in England. This was as part of a disruptive exercise and a way of funding the treasury as well as their own personal businesses, making them some of the wealthiest families in England. After the demise of their father, William (the younger), took over the business at home whilst his brother John took care of the ships and securing trade in Africa and the Caribbean Seas. This is the period that we focus on here.

John Hawkins first got hold of the idea of trafficking Africans from Africa in order to work in the West Indies, from the Spanish, whilst dealing in the arms trade and fitting up ships for voyages, in the Canary Islands. He came to the conclusion that the Spanish colonies in the Americas were short of labour and England and rest of Europe was short of produce. He aimed to kidnap and then enslave Africans by force and provide a cheap (free) work force, making huge profits from the produce. So, the plan was set into motion in the 1560's. Hawkins got together some financial backing for his first voyage in 1562 from some London merchants, government officials and a nod from Queen Elizabeth I. There were two other voyages to follow after this one; all told covering a period of two to three years.

On the first voyage, in October 1562 - August 1563, Hawkins sailed to Guinea/Cape Verde and kidnapped between 300 - 400 Africans, with the help of some local warlords, which involved massacres and the killing of twice to three times this number in the process. To make up numbers, Hawkins made military attacks on Portuguese ships that already had enslaved Africans on board. He then proceeded to Hispaniola/Cuba, where he sold his human cargo in exchange for produce and treasures. On his return home his bounty was well rewarded financially, making quite a substantial profit. This was well received by his investors as every single one made a good profit and were ready to finance his next trip without hesitation.

This second voyage was well sponsored and even the Queen who had been, at first, reticent due to the nature of cargo, endorsed this trip by providing Hawkins the use of her own ship the "Good Ship Jesus" for the voyage. It should be noted that by the last years of her reign, Elizabeth I expressed her disquiet about the numbers of blacks settling in England: 'There are lately blackamoores brought into this realm, of which kind there are already too many.[3] She licensed a Lübeck merchant to ship them to Liberia.

Armed with Royal approval, Hawkins obtained the services of his second cousin Francis Drake who was just starting out as a seafaring apprentice. He was placed on one of the ships to help captain on this voyage and thus started a long term association between the cousins which was to last a long time as Drake advanced to become one of the foremost seafarers of his era.

This 1564-1565 voyage took them to Sierra Leone this time, repeating the previous excessive use of force and amassing a huge human cargo bound for the Americas. More profit and wealth created and attained. He was on a roll and with his cousin Drake now a career seaman, they decided to go for the hat-trick; a third voyage was organized and not too long after the last one.

September of 1565 to October 1569 was the duration of this third expedition. But they were to encounter trouble as they sailed to the Caribbean from the Spanish. It was illegal under Spanish law to traffic people, in all Spanish ports and subsequently, they were arrested, their ships and human cargo impounded and all sailors also detained. Hawkins managed to get his ships and sailors released by pretending to have crossed over and in support of the King of Spain, Philip II. Relationships were sour between Britain and Spain at this time. Hawkins with a little greasing of palms and calling in favours, managed to escape but not with all the ships. Obviously the human cargo had been disposed of. Enough was carried in the few remaining ships to still provide profit for the investors. But this voyage soured further the already fractured relationship between the two countries and is believed to be what eventually led to war between the two countries in 1588 (Spanish Armada) Drake had been involved here as well.

It is said that there were other traders in England that dealt in enslaved Africans before Hawkins and Drake. Two names have been associated with trade namely, John Lok, who brought five enslaved people from Guinea to England in 1555 and William Towerson, whose ships sailed from Plymouth to the African west coast in 1557 and later on in 1569, returning with human cargo. However, Hawkins' is famed for having been the pioneer and father of the Triangular Trade among the English seafarers.

Quote from the BBC History documentary dated - 17th Dec 2011 says:

> *"Hawkins had proved that it was possible to extend the triangular trade between Britain, West Africa and Brazil to a new and potentially valuable commodity i.e. [ENSLAVED AFRICAN]. And it was not an impediment to success in British society. Within a few decades of his death, Britain had joined the Portuguese, Dutch and French, as leading European slave traders."*

For his services, Hawkins was rewarded and his career did not end here as he was to become a Rear Admiral during the war of 1588 and due to his designs and ingenuity, making the British fleet faster and more manoeuvrable, thus able to defeat the much bigger and superior Spanish fleet, Rear Admiral Hawkins was knighted and later appointed as the Naval Commander. Drake was never far from the action either as it seems these cousins were born to the sea. Drake in turn during the in-between years had made his own expeditions and became one of the first seafarers to circumnavigate the globe and his hate for the Spanish led to a life long vow to avenge for the treatment they got on their voyages with cousin Hawkins, he was also a rear admiral during the war with the Spanish.

Hawkins and Drake, were inseparable throughout to the end. They even helped found a charity known as the Chatham Chest, to provide social insurance for injured, disabled and elderly retired sailors in Greenwich.

Hawkins life came to an end whilst doing what he loved doing but this time as part of treasure hunt expedition, organized by cousin Drake in order to attack and raid Spanish ports and ships. The reason being that the trade in the Americas of humans was so lucrative and emboldened by the defeat of the Armada, Britain wanted a proper foothold in the region. This expedition met with heavy defeat and some sailors contracted disease, namely dysentry. Whilst fighting off the cost of Puerto Rico, Hawkins got infected and died soon after in December 1595 and Drake is said to have succumbed to the same illness and his death followed suit in January 1596. This expedition opened the door for a free for all on the Spanish ships carrying treasure and advanced piracy in the Caribbean seas to a new level involving most of the western European countries and some Scandinavian countries too.

As laudable and as feted as these two cousins were and are to this present day, it is quite definite that they were and are responsible for ushering in an era of trade in human cargo (Human Trafficking) that was to last over 200 years. The single most destructive and most unadulterated, most heinous crime ever to befall any race since and ever since.

It should be noted that these two English gentlemen, John Hawkins and Sir Francis Drake were pillars of English society at the time and were part of wealthy/rich gentry. This makes one wonder what type of society that was and the legacy that they left. We understand that the family continued in the same trade, as it was their chosen trade; Hawkins' son, Richard Hawkins took over the reins. This was a trade of enslaving innocent people and using them as a means to national/private gain and profit and was the backbone of most businesses and treasurer's coffers of most countries in Western Europe at the time. It also seems that most of the trading done by these families was not of a legitimate nature; piracy and trade in innocent humans and all legitimized with Royals and their Privy Council approval. What indeed was the moral gauge of the time, if any?

So were they heroes or crooks? If you agree in human trafficking then they are heroes as they were very good at it, but if you are against human trafficking and enslavement then they are definitely crooks.

What has come to be referred to as "The Good Ship Jesus" was in fact the "Jesus of Lubeck," a 700-ton ship purchased by King Henry VIII from the Hanseatic League, a merchant alliance between the cities of Hamburg and Lubeck in Germany. Twenty years after its purchase the ship, in disrepair, was lent to Sir John Hawkins by Queen Elizabeth.

Reference: https://kathrynmckinney.wordpress.com/2013/04/25/the-good-ship-jesus-the-beginning-of-the-slave-trade/

East African enslaved children taken aboard HMS Daphne

Hawkins was quite unashamed of the source of his wealth. He adopted the above as his crest this is a figure of a bound enslaved human being.

African enslaved people (children) in Islamic Lands (Also let us not forget the Arab enslavement of Africans)

Notes & References:
Miscellaneous on Google history - John Hawkins bio, facts etc.
www.blacknetworkinggroup
John Hawkins Answers.com

Dismemberment of Memory

In this section I quote very heavily from the political thinker and writer Ngũgĩ wa Thiong' o. In his book 'Remembering Africa' Thiong' o states that when the British finally caught the Kenyan freedom fighter Waiyaki wa Hinga, they removed him from his region, the base of his power and on the way to the Kenya coast buried him alive at Kibwezi, head facing the bowels of the earth. This was in opposition to his cultural Gikuyu burial rites, which requires his body to face Mount Kenya, where they believe the Supreme deity dwells.[4]

In South Africa when the British captured the freedom fighter Xhosa king Hintsa, they decapitated him and took his head to the British Museum for display. A similar type of decapitating and lynching was also taking place in the USA during slavery and the Jim Crow era, usually African male genitalia were cut off and displayed as trophies and in some cases eaten by their white tormentors. Why was this done? Thiong' o goes on to say that, as well as triumph and humiliation, he believes it to be a part of social engineering. It was one of the tactics used to keep the mind of a once free people enslaved and colonized.[5]

The word dismemberment, according to Wikipedia, means:

> "an act of cutting, tearing, pulling, wrenching or otherwise removing the limbs of a living thing. It has been practised upon human beings as a form of capital punishment, can occur as a result of a traumatic accident..."

The continent Africa, suffered dismemberment not

only of its physical body but also of its mind. It has taken effect in two ways; first by the kidnapping of millions of people and forcefully taking them thousands of miles from their homelands, to work on plantations for free. Helping to create enough wealth to finance the industrial revolution, but would also open the idea of creating new markets to sell finished products. This gave rise to the second dismemberment of Africa when western European countries met in Berlin in 1884-85 and decided to carve up Africa for themselves. So we can see that the Africans who were now in diaspora separated from their home-lands, their labour and even their own minds.

Whilst the Africans at home were now on plantations which were once their homes and as in the diaspora separated from their labour and minds, just like the enslaved in the Caribbean the African at home under a colonial state has no longer any say over the affairs of his land or labour. He is now a colonized subject and has no say over his produce but must take orders from his colonial master. Once his own man and now he is a man owned.

It is during this dismemberment that the African was made to forget who he/she was. The removing of Hintsa's head and placing it on display at the British Museum could be symbolic of removing the African memory from the masses of the people.[6] The renaming of people and places such as the new world renamed and called America, New Hispaniola in the Caribbean, Zimbabwe becomes Rhodesia, Ghana becomes Gold coast, Namlolwe (Lake East Africa) becomes Lake Victoria and Kunta Kinte becomes Toby Waller.

The Desire to Read and Write During Enslavement

Most slave owners needed Africans just for labour on their plantations, so having an African learn to read and write in the Caribbean was not necessary and in fact most slave owners deemed that to be dangerous. An enslaved African who could read and write would be able to read documents the slave owner did not want him to see, be able to communicate his/ her ideas to other enslaved Africans, able to teach other enslaved Africans to read and write and most importantly would be able to plan an escape and plot a rebellion against the slave owner. The penalty of catching an enslaved African reading or learning how to read could be death.

The Creation of Ujima (Collective Work and Responsibility)

After emancipation in the Caribbean, Africans had to start from the very bottom; they had no money, no land, no housing, no job and up until then, denied the opportunity for over 200 years to read and write by their former slave masters. Many of them did not even have any clothing to wear, Africans were truly in an extremely desperate condition. In his book 'To Shoot hard Labour' Samuel Smith recalls that many of the people of Antigua just after emancipation, were literally living in the mud[7]. They received little to no help from England, unlike their former slave master, who received compensation from the English government for loss of income. Also their former slave masters made life very difficult for them to earn a living income, get access to land, property and even to eat. This was so that they would be forced to go back on the plantations to work for nothing or very little. You must understand that the planters were very upset in that what they believed was their property, the enslaved Africans, was no longer theirs and so they no longer had a free labour force, an amazing asset that was continually bringing in huge amounts of passive income for them.

Despite all the hardship Africans faced post emancipation they still had their inventive and creative mind intact and with this they got together and created their own types of co-operatives very similar to the East African system of Kawaida, from which in the late part of the 20th century Dr Maulana Karenga studied and derived the Kwanzaa celebration (First Fruits) and the Nguzo Saba (Seven Life Principles); they engaged and used seven of the principles, which Karenga would formulate into a system 130 years later. Three of these I shall highlight, they are 'Ujima' which translates to Collective Work and Responsibility and 'Ujamaa' which is Cooperative Economics, these two are bound together by the first principle of the Nguzo Saba 'Umoja' which means Unity. These principles the African used just after emancipation to take themselves out of their wretched conditions. For examples they helped build each others housing, they helped each other cultivate their land and they set up their own banking systems called Pardners, Partners or Susu (Keithlyn Smith 1985).

The Colour Bar

During 1700s in Britain, a type of Black Code law existed, similar to the ones created in the USA after 1865. According to J.A. Rodgers, it was evoked in 1731, 'the Lord Mayor and Aldermen of that city [London] decreed that no Negroes should be taught trades.' It's quite ironic that during the same period, in Britain an African invented the first 'fine needle'.[8]

In the 1940s at the height of the Second World War 8,000 West Indian troops had joined the war effort in Britain, whilst racism in its most brazen in its most brazen form was being supported at the highest levels.[9] In 1942 the British Cabinet discussed the proposals to endorse the colour bar so as to avoid offending the racist sensibilities of white American troops. After an incident where a black official at the Colonial Office was barred from a restaurant because of the objections of American troops, the Prime minister at the time Winston Churchill when was told about this, responded saying "That's alright, if he takes his banjo with him they'll think that he's one of the band!"[10]

When we speak of racial discrimination of black or darker skinned people by white people, we often think of 1950/60 America and the civil rights movement or 1948 to 1994 Apartheid South Africa, but seldom do we speak of Britain in the same way. Most people born after the 1980s will not know much or even have heard of the term colour bar in the UK. Prior to the late 1970s the colour bar was quite common in Britain, for example, it was not a rare sight for black people to see in house window's signs that said 'no blacks, no dogs and no Irish', when looking for accommodation to rent. Things were no better when trying to get employment.

In the book 'The Windrush Legacy-Memories of Britain's Post-War Caribbean Immigrants' the authors quote that "Only 13% West Indian men, and 5% of West Indian women, who came to Britain during the 1950s had no skills. Half of the women and a quarter of the men were non-manual workers. Almost half of the men (46%) and a quarter of the women (27%) were skilled manual workers. But despite their skills they were usually given the worst jobs; these were the jobs most English (white) people refused to do. In the late 1950s more than 50% of West Indian men in London had lower-status jobs than their skills."[11]

These types of descriptions caused blacks living in Britain to take action. According to an article on Wikipedia, a bus boycott broke out in 1963 in Bristol city because of the refusal of the Bristol Omnibus Company to employ black or Asian as bus crews in the city. The boycott was led by youth worker Paul Stephenson and the West Indian Development Council, it lasted for four months until the bus company backed down on its racist policy. Many believe that the Bristol Bus Boycott gave rise to the Race Relations Act of 1965, which was strengthened in 1968 and again in the late 1970s with the Race Relations Act of 1976. This led to the creation of the organization the Commission for Racial Equality, known as 'CRE'.

Bristol Bus Boycott

Lazima Tutashinda Bilashaka – A Luta Continua

We have made great progress as a 'black community' in the UK - the term 'community' here, is loosely used, and the explanation as to why, is beyond the scope of this book, but that progress has been made, is undeniable and the evidence, definitely, empirical.

Our positive contributions can be felt all over the UK. But it's our opinion that we still have a very long way to go in the UK. As black people we must decide if the UK is going to be the home of our future generations and if so, are we happy to be completely assimilated within the majority society or will we take a note from other successful UK communities such as the Jewish and Indian communities, who arguably, have done very well in the UK whilst holding on to their culture and religions. Their contributions are not only felt in the British culture but can be seen in the buildings and monuments which they have erected for example; schools, synagogues, temples, banks and other places of work etc.

It's our belief that black children in the UK have good role model examples to follow in terms of continuing our progress and development in the UK. We have the historical examples of our ancestors, who toiled the fields of the Caribbean under enslavement, but fought to free themselves and succeeded.

Also our ancestors on the continent who fought to free themselves of colonialism and also succeeded. And even the ancestors brought to these shores, as enslaved, managed to free themselves over time and through sheer determination.

We must stop feeling ashamed of slavery, we continue to hear some 'black' folk say that " I don't want to know about the enslavement of African people.." Some believe that it was in the past and so say "...let's just forget it and let's live now in the present", whilst others says, ".. Yeah, I know about slavery but we also had a glorious history before that..." Although they are both right to some degree, as yes, we did have a glorious past before our enslavement by both the Arabs and Europeans. We should live in the present as it is the most important time period, but we have to understand that the present is directly connected to the past which in turn is connected to the future. We can't have a collective future if we can't deal with our collective past.

Instead of feeling ashamed of our enslavement, we should draw strength and wisdom from it. Let's not forget that Africans resisted their enslavement in various forms which included riots, rebellions and revolutions, until finally they forced the European powers involved in the evil trade to release them.

This history of fighting for freedom and self-determination must not be forgotten.

Important Words from Marcus Garvey.

The great leader of African people throughout the world the honourable Marcus Garvey who once lived and in fact spent his last days in England, said in one of his speeches that

'... ***We must teach our children to become Scientists & [Inventors] par excellence as it is only through science that we will defeat the evil effects of modern materialism...'***

What did he mean by this? I don't believe enough of us have taken the time to understand what he actually meant by those words.

Frederick Douglas
The Great African American Abolitionist

Douglas once said that

> "Those who profess to favour freedom and yet depreciate agitation, are people who want crops without ploughing the ground; they want rain without thunder and lightning; they want the ocean without the roar of its many waters. The struggle may be a moral one, or it may be a physical one, or it may be both. But it must be a struggle. Power concedes nothing without a demand. It never did and it never will."

I want these words to burn into the minds of our young people, as everywhere that I have studied the plight of African people, and in fact, other people who have been wronged, the only time I have seen any real change, is not when they are given freedom or independence, but when they have demanded it and were willing to take any form of negative consequence.

Booker T. Washington - The Great African - American Industrialist, educator, author, orator, and advisor to presidents of the United States

Frederick Douglass The Great African - American Social Reformer, Orator, Writer, and Statesman

In the late 1800s, just 20 years after his own emancipation from enslavement, Booker T. Washington went on to set up the Tuskegee Institute, an industrial school, where he taught recently freed Africans in America, nation building skills which included all the sciences. A school that taught the value of labour, and being independent and self sufficient. The school produced some of the greatest African American industrialist, scientists and inventors. They also employed talented black professors one of these was amongst America's greatest scientists and Inventors, Dr. George Washington Carver. He was the inventor of over 300 products which were extracted from the peanut, sweet potato and the soya bean. His discoveries and inventions helped to revolutionize the American agricultural industry of the late 1800s and early 1900s. Carver himself was freed from slavery after the emancipation proclamation in 1865. The example of the work of Booker T. Washington and George Carver during the 19th Century would have not only been influential on other African Americans, but it would have also had a huge impact on Africans in the Caribbean and those in Africa. After all the great leader, Marcus Garvey from Jamaica, was inspired to start his life's work after reading Booker T. Washington's autobiography "Up From Slavery".

In his book Washington points out how he and those that were enslaved before him had to give their labour for free for over 200 years building up a country that was cruel and wicked to his people. But now that they are free they should use their own labour to build communities, which are better for them and their families. The author concurs with this point simply because there still is racism around; people who would rather lie than tell the truth and delight in telling lies that African people are lazy. How can a people that worked up to seven days a week, twelve to fourteen hours a day, for over 200 years for free, whilst their captors sat idle exerting very little labour energy, be lazy.

There is evidence in America that Africans during slavery were rented from plantation to plantation, not only to tend to crop such as cotton, coffee or sugar cane, but also to build the planters mansions. Case in point the American white house, where enslaved African's from the southern states, were hired out to the north to build the presidential palace, and many more examples. And let's not forget that an ex enslaved African called Benjamin Banneker one of America's fathers of mathematics and an inventor of a clock, made totally out of wood, helped design the capital state of America, Washington D.C., in the 1700s. There are very few books and fewer TV documentaries that show these hidden facts. The case is similar in the Caribbean where enslaved Africans were rented out to across the island plantations and further still to other islands. So we can see that Africans both laboured with their body and brains for the purpose of others. This work ethic was then instilled into their children generations after slavery Who in turn would have eventually brought it with them years later from the Caribbean as they immigrated to the UK.

The Same Story In The Caribbean

In the Caribbean there was a group of white men who came from European countries such as England, as mechanics, who earned no considerable respect in their native land, but in Caribbean counties, because of their skin colour, they had put themselves in the exploitative class. Not quite as high as the plantocracy but higher than the enslaved Africans and indentured white labour. But these men did not have skills that were useful within the Caribbean[12] . In his book, The African Inventor in the New World and His Contribution to Technology, Medicine and Science, Dr. John Henrik Clarke writes:

> '...The enslaved African craftsmen begun to replace them. We see the beginnings of the Africans' inventive mind in the Caribbean Islands. The same thing was happening in parts of South America. Many times the English would bring over English-made furniture and there were some termites in the Caribbean. Some of these termites are still there, and when the termites began to eat up the softwood in the English-made furniture, the African with his meticulous mind began to duplicate that furniture with local hard wood. This was done especially in Jamaica where they [once] had large amounts of mahogany...'

Due to their skills these African craftsmen were given a degree of freedom and they were paid wages. They were allowed to move around their islands, travel abroad to places such as the US and even back to Africa. Please note this was at a time when Africans in the Caribbean were denied the right to learn how to read and write, a law that existed in the Caribbean for over 200 years. At this time in the Caribbean the quickest way for the ex-enslaved African to elevate himself and his family economically was to become skilled in the crafts. As the colonies became sophisticated urban and rural communities, skilled [enslaved Africans] were put in charge of other areas of the economy, such as artisan work, transport or clerical task.[13]

During the early 19th century it was these Africans that travelled to England to seek either higher education or better employment opportunities.

The Africans Bring Electricity and Light To England

As a student of electricity and electronics, I don't think I ever came across any single book in school, college or university, on the contributions that Lewis Howard Latimer (the son of a run-away slave) made to the British electrical industry.

Lewis Latimer invented a light bulb, using the carbon filament principle and also the machinery to manufacture it. He also, in 1874, co-invented (with Charles W. Brown), an improved toilet system for railroad cars, called the Water Closet for Rail road Cars (U.S. Patent 147,363) and in 1876, Alexander Graham Bell employed Latimer, then a draughtsman, at Bell's patent law firm, to draft the necessary drawings required to receive a patent for Bell's telephone. In 1879, he was working for U.S. Electric Lighting Company, a company owned by Hiram Maxim.

He was asked to join Hiram Maxim in London England, to help set up the early electrical industry in the England.

From 1882 Latimer lived in London with his wife for about one year before returning to America. Latimer's work at the time in the electric lamp and the early electrical industry at that time was revolutionary, his writings were published in many of the top electrical journals. I wonder what children (in particular black children) in the UK would think about black peoples intellect, if they were taught in both history and physics classes about this man's contributions to physics and electronics.

Lewis Howard Latimer 1848 - 1928

Notes & References:
1. African People European Holidays Vol II, pg 33. | 2. Ibid pp 34. | 3. The Trader,The Owner, The Slave, Walvin, pg 181. | 4. Re-membering Africa' Thiong' o, pg 1. | 5. Ibid pp 2 – 4. | 6. Ibid pp, pg 9. | 7. To Shoot hard Labour' Smith, pg 162. | 8. Sex & Race Vol 1, Rodgers, pg 201. | 9. The Windrush Legacy-Memories of Britain's Post-War Caribbean Immigrants, BCA, London, 1998) pg 21. | 10. Ibid pp 21. | 11. Ibid pp 41. | 12. The African Inventor in the New World and His Contribution to Technology, Medicine and Science, pg 66. | 13. The Trader,The Owner, The Slave, Walvin, pg 184.

Web References:
Miscellaneous on Google history - John Hawkins bio, facts etc. | www. blacknetworkinggroup | John Hawkins Answers.com

Time Line 2 - Middle History

Time Line 2
Middle History

- **55 B.C.E. -** Romans enter Britian led by General (Emperor) Julius Caesar.

- **43 B.C.E. -** Romans enter Britain again led by Emperor Claudius he is met with fierce resistance from the Black Silures who live in Briton.

- **79 C.E. -** Britain becomes a province of Rome.

- **122-128 C.E. -** Hadrian's Wall is built by the Romans.

- **146 C.E. -** Emperor Septimius Severus is born in Africa. This African later becomes emperor of the Roman empire.

- **176 C.E.** Emperor Septimius Severus (The African) rules Britain (he supervises the restoration of Hadrian's Wall).

- **2/3rd - 7th C.E. -** The Moors enter northern Britain they influence the Briton's culture with their advance civilization, culture, arts and science.

- **757 C.E. -** Anglo Saxon tribe from Saxony in Germany enter Britain. (Alfred the Great is their king)

- **8th - 19th century -** The Arab En-Slavement Trade. Claimed to have been bigger than the trans-atlantic trade, covered 1100 years totaling 8 - 12million enslaved peoples over the duration. Trade mainly in the Indian ocean, the red sea and the Mediterranean sea. Run mainly by the sultanate of Oman that had an empire/ caliphates covering a vast area - from Atlantic western Europe, most of Asian continent and to the far east. In Africa this covered the horn of Africa and the eastern African coast all the way to Mozambique with his HQ base on Zanzibar Island. Non - discriminatory - he had slaves from Europe/Asia/Africa/ & even Scandinavian countries, all feeding the vast Arab market. Most famous trader in Indian ocean was Tippu Tip. No abolition dates given but superseded by trans - Atlantic enslavement trade as it proved more lucrative.

- **907-1005 C.E.** - King Kenneth III, is the last King of Scotland

- **1066 C.E.** - The Normans invade Britain from France - under William the conquer.

- **1457-1509** - African Moors in England during the Tudor Times (both enslaved and free persons).

- **1492** - Christopher Colon Columbus, claims to discover the Americas (Caribbean Islands) whilst looking westwards for India.

- **1507** - John 'Blacke the trumpet' is part of King Henry VIII's, trumpeters

- **1507** - Martin Waldseemuller, a German Cartographer gives the mainland the name America in honour of Italian sailor Amerigo Vespucci.

- **1555** - John Lok brings over five Ghanians, prior to the British involvement in trans-Atlantic Enslavement Trade.

- **1562** - Admiral John Hawkins kidnapped 300 people from the Guinea coast in Africa, took them to the Caribbean Island of Hispaniola and sold them to the Spaniards for £10,0000 worth of pearls, hides, sugar and ginger. He a made 12% return on this investment. At first Queen Elizabeth disproves of this saying ***"It's detestable and will call down vengeance from Heaven upon the undertakers"*** But once she sees his profits, she quickly changes her opinion, becomes a share holder and blesses him with the use of her ship [The Good Ship Jesus] to traffic Africans on his next trip.

- **1566** - Hawkin's cousin, France Drake (later knighted), also gets involved in human trafficking of Africans and piracy.

- **1570s -** Africans now brought to England as a by product to slavery.

- **1579 -** Drake claims California for England and names it New Albion (New England)

- **1700s -** John Edmonstone is born in Guyana

- **1702 -** Francis Williams is born in Jamaica

- **1729 -** George Bridgetower is born, excellent musician and conductor who worked with Beethoven, worked in London and Europe, dies in Peckham.

- **1743 -** Olaudah Equianio is born in (Nigeria) Africa, and kidnapped circa 1753.

- **1757 -** Ottobah Cugoano is born in (Ghana) Africa, and kidnapped circa 1772.

- **1764 -** Africans help both the colonist (later called Americans) and loyalist (the British) in the American War For Independence as they were promised their freedom. Africans who fought with the British during the American War of Independence, settle in England after.

- **1770 -** (circa) Francis Williams dies

- **1783 -** The captain of the ship 'the Zong' carrying 470 kidnapped Africans, from Africa to Jamaica, murders 132 sick Africans on board, in order that he and sponsors to realize maximum profits.

- **1787 -** The black poor of London (many were ex-army and served along side the English) were deported to Sierra lone.

- **1795 -** Dr. Richard Hart is born in Jamaica.

- **1803 -** The Haitian Revolution - Africans fight the British, Spanish, Americans and French and free themselves of enslavement on the Island of Haiti. (For this act they would be punished by the aforementioned countries economically to this very day)

- **1805 -** Mary Seacole is born in Jamaica

- **1807 -** The kidnapping and trafficking of Africans from Africa is made illegal within the British Empire.

- **1816 -** The Barbados Rebellion led by Bussa and Nanny Grigg.

- **1823 -** The Demerara Rebellion (Guyana) led by Quamina.

- **1825 -** Dr. Charles Darwin confesses how John Edmonstone an ex-enslaved African from Guyana teaches him taxidermy.

- **1831/32 -** The Jamaican Rebellion led Samuel Sharpe between December and January of that year. Most of the western side of the Island is torn down by Africans trying to free themselves from European en-slavers. It's believed that all previous rebellions, including this which by far, was the largest in British Caribbean, forced parliament to pass the Abolition law of 1834.

- **1834 -** Britain declares Emancipation for Africans in Caribbean Islands which are part of her empire (On August 1), this includes those in Canada, Mauritius and Capetown in South Africa. August 1st, was a Bank Holiday in Britain for many years, until for no apparent reason, its was moved to the last Monday in October, now known for its display of singing and dancing at Notting Hill Carnival.

- **1834 -** Although parliament under the British legal system makes the bondage of Africans illegal, Africans in the Caribbean have to work an extra four years if they are 'House Slaves' or 6 years if they are 'Field Slaves', this was called the Apprenticeship System, it was a sneaky way to get/squeeze more money from the labour of the enslaved Africans in the Caribbean as the system was being dismantled.

- **1834** - Planters such as Sir Edward Codrington and Sir. John Gladstone (Father of 4 x British Prime Minsters, William Gladstone (1809-1898)) plus many more including 100 Members of the Houses of Parliament (1820 to1835) and 160 Church of England ministers, are compensated to the tune of £20 million (equivalent to £20 billion today) for loss of earnings due to having to release - under duress - Africans in the Caribbean. This compensation went to fund Art collections, build infrastructure in Briton, including roads and railway systems, funding British scientists such as James Watt, the inventor of the steam train etc.

- **1835** - Dr. James Africanus Beale Horton is born in Sierra Leone

- **1838** - After intense fighting against the British Planters(enslavers), Africans in the Caribbean finally win some form of Emancipation.

- **1846** - Dr. Richard Hill helps English scientist Phillip Gosse whilst Gosse on visit to Jamaica.

- **1854** - Mary Seacole from Jamaica arrives in Britain, to help treat British soldiers with her remedies in the Crimea.

- **1863** - Dr. James S.R. Russel is born in Guyana?

- **1865** - the Morant Bay Rebellion

- **1865** - The Emancipation Proclamation in the USA.

- **1872** - Dr. Richard Hart dies

- **1875** - Samuel Coleridge-Taylor, outstanding African musician is born in Holborn, London.

- **1881** - Mary Seacole dies in London.

- **1882** - Dr. James Jackson Brown dies.

- **1883** - Dr. James Africanus Beal Horton dies.

- **1885 -** The Berlin Conference and the scramble for Africa. Several western European countries decided to carve up Africa for themselves.

- **1879 -** King Cetawayo and his Zulu soldiers fight the British in South Africa, in order to keep their lands and halt enslavement of the Zulu. Many Planters (slave-masters) in the Caribbean who believe that they too have an interest in South Africa, travel to help the British defeat the Zulus, before returning back to their plantations. The Zulu's kill 1400 British troops.

- **1873 -** Dr. John Alcindor is born in Trinidad and Tobago

- **1882 -** Dr. Harold Moody is born in Jamaica

- **1882 -** Dr. James Jackson Brown born in St. Thomas, Jamaica

- **1900s and 1940s -** Africans emigrated/recruited to Britain to help Britain fight in the two World Wars.

- **1907 -** Dr. John Alcindor set up his own practice in Acton, London.

- **1913 -** Dr. Harold Moody creates his 'Open Door' clinic, by setting up his own medical practice at 11 Kings Grove, Peckham, South East, London.

- **1920 -** Dr. Allan Powell Goffe, is born in Kingston-Upon-Thames, UK

- **1920 -** Dr. Sir Arthur Wint was born in Manchester, Jamaica.

- **1924 -** Dr. John Alcindor dies

- **1930 -** Dr. Charles Ssali is born in Uganda

- **1960-64 -** Dr. Alan Powell Goffe involved in international development of polio vaccine, & also developed measles vaccine.

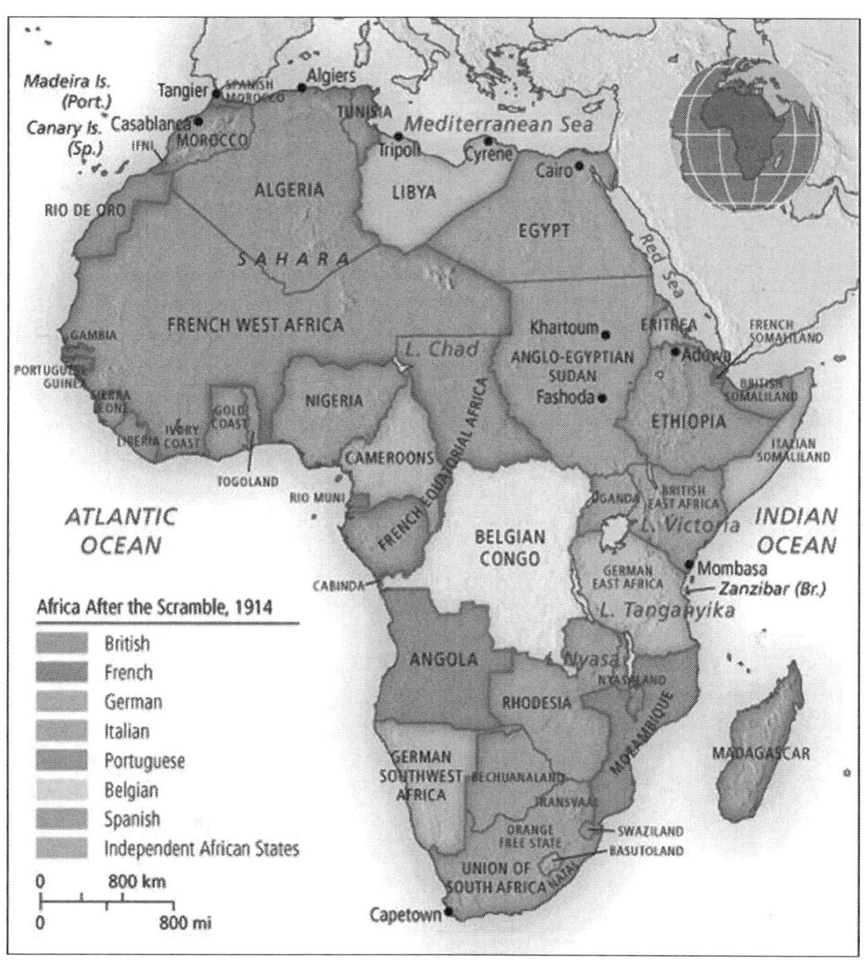

Africa after the Scramble 1914

Make a copy of this greyscale map and with students let them learn by colour coding this map which countries colonised Africa. This will allow a better understanding of contemporary Africa today.

Part V:
Chapter 6 -

Black Scientists & Inventors In Britain Old & Modern

Why Black British Scientists & Inventors?

CHAPTER 6

Black Scientists & Inventors In Britain Old & Modern

Why Black British Scientists & Inventors?

We chose this subject for a number of reasons:

1. The first and most important is that we became literally more than a little tired of hearing, many UK main stream teachers and head teachers (mostly those not of African descent), ask this question, *"Why is it that you don't feature Black British Scientists and Inventors in your publications?" We, in turn would reply with, "but our books do! - although not only do we feature UK scientists and inventors, we also feature African Americans, Africans in the Caribbean, the Pacific, Europe and of course, from the African continent itself."* We then go on to explain the reasons saying, "...there is a connection and shared narrative within the African family. You see when Africans were kidnapped from Africa and then taken to the Americas, during the Trans-Atlantic Enslavement Trade, they may have been incarcerated on one island at first, but it would not have been uncommon, throughout their enslaved lives,

to be ferried between the islands and the American mainland and vice versa. This would have been done by their en-slavers, who may have loaned them out either, as studs, "to work on another planters land, to work off a debt of one planter to another or sold on to another en-slaver."

Again we see the shared histories of Africans after 1838 and 1865 etc as emancipation is finally declared and reaches the Islands and then later on similar freedoms enacted throughout the Americas, we see the early signs of the African family structure trying to rebuild itself. After abduction, family units deliberately and mercilessly, torn apart for over 400 years, we see the African woman in the main, travelling throughout the Caribbean Islands, looking for her Kith and Kin. We also see African men looking for work, which may have meant travelling to another islands or even the American mainland and vice versa, to help maintain these new common unities. We end by pointing out to the teachers that, "...This meant that the African American in reality, was not that different from African Caribbean due to these shared historical experiences ..."

2. On a number of occasions we have been invited to present on the subject of Black Scientists & Inventors, at the London Science Museum. These presentations have always been received well and usually to packed audiences, but on occasions we have also experienced groups of black people who are resistant to our presentations before having seen or even heard the contents. It would seem that they work on assumptions based on, may be, other events they may

have attended or heard of, that may have precluded living and present day black British Scientists and Inventors - surely not ours! But we found that If or when they do attend our presentations, most are pleasantly surprised at the end. That said, we have previously not featured as many as we would have liked to and so this present title has enabled us to do so.

3. Finally, we read a report from research which was carried out in 2012, by the African Heritage Group. It was entitled "How African Heritage is Taught in British Schools", one of its findings was that school teachers, parents and children 'actually wanted to know' about the contributions that African/Caribbean people have made and are still making in the UK. We obliged and indulged ourselves.

The Black Inventor Who Excluded Himself From This Book.

In all the years in which we have been involved in producing the best-selling Black Scientists and Inventors series of books, we had never received a refusal from a black scientist or inventor whom we wanted featured in those titles. That was until asking a young extremely talented black British inventor if he would like to be featured in this title, he replied NO. When we asked him why he did not want to be included? He replied in an e-mail that he did not want to be included in a publication just about the contributions of black people, but would rather be included in a title based on merit. We must say that we were a little taken back with his response. At first we really wondered whether he had seen or ever read any of the Black Scientists & Inventors titles already in the public domain? Otherwise why would he think we would only include people in our series based on colour? What a massive assumption he had made. We also wondered to ourselves why he could not see that one of the main reasons we contacted him was due his outstanding work amongst his peers. It's our opinion that he could not see the bigger picture, it's not that we think that we shouldn't be judged on merit, of course we should, but we are also aware of our history and the hundreds of years of negative propaganda that has been used against us and has gone a long way to arrest our development. And so we have to recognize the importance of challenging these negative propaganda by producing positive, accurate and truthful information about our achievements. We know, by first hand experience, what the effects are to a young mind (also older ones) when he/she sees someone who looks like them produce or invent a product that is useful. When a young person sees that as well as being a great athlete or rapper he/she can also be a great inventor or scientist, this opens their mind to a new reality, widens their world view and informs them of all possibilities. It is our hope that one day this young black inventor would realize just how important he and his inventions are, to all people of the world in general, and to young black [British] people in particular.

All the chapters up to this point were to set the scene of what we are about to present. We painstakingly researched for more than three years the contributions that people of Africans descent have made to the UK, in the arena of science and inventions. It is our pleasure to present our findings, which are the biographies of 35 scientists and inventors of African origin that have in some way contributed positively to the landscape of the United Kingdom.

Dr. Samantha Tross

***"Reach for the stars...
You just have to have self-belief.
Expect knock backs. It will be
part of the course. If you expect
them, then when they inevitably
occur, you are not stressed or
disappointed."***

- Samantha Tross

John Edmonstone

(1700 circa)

Taxidermy is the art of preparing, stuffing, and mounting the skins of animals for display for scientific studies, hunting trophies, or other sources of study. Taxidermy can be done on all vertebrate species of animals, including mammals, birds, fish, reptiles, and amphibians. A person who practices taxidermy is called a taxidermist. To become skilled in taxidermy, the taxidermist should be very familiar with anatomy, sculpture, painting, and tanning.

Freed enslaved Guyanese African John Edmonstone had learnt the art of taxidermy from the naturalist Charles Waterton. John Edmonstone was born in the 1700s, probably in Demerara, Guyana. In 1807, Edmonstone's master brought him to Edinburgh and freed him. He settled in a house a few doors down from Charles and Erasmus Darwin.

Charles Darwin, the famous English scientist, received Edmonstone's tuition in taxidermy, natural studies, and scientific information about the flora and fauna of the South American continent between February and April 1826. How do we know this? Darwin had written to his sister, "I am going to learn to stuff birds from a blackamoor." Also, in Darwin's autobiography, he writes about Edmonstone while a student at Edinburgh between October 1825 and April 1827: "A negro lived in Edinburgh, who had travelled with Waterton, and gained his livelihood by stuffing birds, which he did excellently; he gave me lessons for payment and I often used to sit with him for he was a pleasant and intelligent man."

The knowledge that Edmonstone imparted to Darwin would become very important in Darwin's later work in areas such as recording of bird and animal life during his voyage with the H.M.S. Beagle in 1831 and his study of the Galapagos finches, as well as contributing to the significant collections that he made while travelling. All of these may have informed, to a great extent, his theory of evolution.

One can argue that it was Charles Darwin's encounter with John Edmonstone at the University of Edinburgh that set Darwin on the anti-slavery course when many of his contemporary scientists who passed through the same halls in Edinburgh took the reverse course.

Summary

John Edmonstone developed his skill to such a high level that he became in high demand, teaching both teachers and scientists the art of Taxidermy.

References:
http://en.wikipedia.org/wiki/Taxidermy
https://royalsociety.org/exhibitions/2012/black-history-month/working-in-the-background/ (Jide Uwechia), http://www.africaresource.com/rasta/sesostris-the-great-the-egyptian-hercules/john-edmonstone-the-black-genius-who-schooled-charles-darwin-by-jide-uwechia/

Francis Williams

(1702 - 1770 circa)

Francis Williams was born in 1702, to John and Dorothy Williams, a free black couple living in Jamaica. He lived in the Caribbean at a time when the enslavement of Africans was producing huge profits for England, which relied on slave labour to produce sugar, coffee, cotton, and ink.

John and Dorothy Williams' reasonable wealth and their stability of not being enslaved meant that they could afford to send Francis away to receive an education. In 1716, whilst in pursuit of good education, the governor of the island, the Duke of Montague, helped send Williams to England where he enrolled at a grammar school; he later entered the University of Cambridge, where he made considerable progress in mathematics and other branches of science. He also excelled in the study of the classics, an essential part of the education of an 18th century gentleman. Some historians say that Williams was a social experiment of the Duke of Montague as he wanted to prove that the black man could equal a white man if given the same education and opportunity.

Williams was an excellent poet of Latin verses and odes and also held political aspirations. According to the Royal Society, his aspirations were, however, frequently denied; his election to the Royal Society - appearing as a single line in the archives - was refused. In an article in the Gentleman's Magazine from May 1771, an unnamed author wrote that the refusal was "on account of his complexion."

In a painting that can be seen at Victoria and Albert Museum, Williams is depicted in a contemporary portrait standing amongst objects of his learning: books, a globe, and a telescope. He is also fashionably and expensively dressed, every bit the eminent man of culture and science. He can also be seen resting his hand on a book entitled Newton's Philosophy.

After spending several years in England, Williams returned to Jamaica, where the Duke of Montague offered him a post on the council that advised the governor, but this offer did not materialise. With financial help from the governor, Williams opened a school in Spanish Town, where he taught reading, writing, Latin, and the elements of mathematics. Because of his Cambridge education, as well as teaching freed blacks who would have been hungry for an education, both coloureds and poor whites sought his teachings.

Williams also had his detractors; white author Edward Long tried to undermine Williams' ability and that of the entire African race in his writings. Despite the deep prejudices held against him because of the colour of his skin, which would prevent him from taking up his deserved place in science and society, Francis Williams' successes in mathematics and verse earned him recognition amongst many people.

Summary

Francis Williams went to the highest levels of the British education system, also attending Cambridge one of its best universities. And do remember this was at least 80 years before slavery ended in the Caribbean and over 100 years before it ended in the USA. William's life did demonstrate that if anyone is given opportunities and that person is willing to take the opportunity with drive and ambition they can be successful at anything. Williams again was one who did not pull up the ladder behind him,but instead went back to Jamaica the country of his birth to set up schools to help others.

References:
https://royalsociety.org/exhibitions/2012/black-history-month/working-in-the-background/
http://joyousjam2.tripod.com/jamaicaspioneerteachers/id11.html

Dr. Richard Hill

(1795-1872)

Richard Hill was born in Montego Bay, Jamaica, on 1st May 1795 to an English Planter (possibly a slave owner) and a free African woman. Even though slavery in Jamaica did not officially end until 1838, at the age of five in 1800, Hill was sent over to England to study. He most likely was afforded this opportunity because of his mixed heritage and his wealthy English father.

After Hill finished his academic education in England, he traveled to several countries where he studied the institution of slavery. On his return to England, along with the Anti-Slavery Society, he presented a petition to the House of Commons in favor of the abolition of slavery. He also was involved in delivering presentations to British people on the evils of slavery.

Hill's father's dying wish was for his son to return to Jamaica and help his people. In 1823, at 24 years old, Hill returned to Jamaica to fight against slavery, which continued another 15 years. He also embarked upon a career as a writer, politician, and science researcher.

Hill had an inquisitive mind and was interested in all fields of study. He was particularly interested in the natural sciences. He would often walk along the Jamaican countryside observing and collecting plants and insects. He was interested in how they fed themselves, how they reproduced, and how they aged and died. During his research, Hill was able to discover several animals and plants that had not been previously documented. Due to the pioneering work

Hill was carrying out in Jamaica, word about this work had travelled to many countries.

Scientists in England travelled to Jamaica to meet Hill. Phillip Gosse did so in 1846, and Hill showed Gosse around the island so he could study and write about the birds he saw. Because of the major contribution that Hill provided for Gosse's book Birds of Jamaica, he made Hill the co-author. English scientist Dr. Charles Darwin was also indebted to Richard Hill for his help in supplying him with facts and specimens from Jamaica. In A.S. Johnson's book Great Jamaican Scientists, he writes that "In 1859, when Darwin wrote The Origins of The Species, it was one of the ten most important books of all times. In this book he gives credit to Richard Hill, saying he was 'a most kind and valuable correspondent.'"

Hill was also a very talented artist, and because the the camera had just been invented in the early 1800s, it was not in common use in Jamaica. So Hill sketched all the plant and animal specimens he found for research, and the likeness was excellent. His artwork can be see today in places such as the Institute of Jamaica and amongst natural history collections in the US and Britain.

In 1854, Hill became secretary of the Jamaican Society of Arts, and in 1855, at the request of Governor Henry Barclay, he was asked

Jamaica Long-tailed Humming-bird, male.

to send a collection of Jamaican flora and fauna to the World Exhibition in Paris, France, which at the time was considered to be the European Centre for science and technology. The exhibition showcased specimens from all over the world, and Hill sent over Jamaican specimens accompanied with a catalogue he prepared. Out of the hundreds of specimens sent from every region of the earth, only five gold medals were awarded, and one of the five went to Jamaica because of Hill's work.

In 1857, when a cholera outbreak was creating havoc on the island, Hill's knowledge of botany allowed him to provide a natural remedy from an indigenous plant called the Eupatorium Nervosum (Bitter Bush).

Throughout Hill's life, his work was published in many journals, and the Royal Zoological Society of London, the Academy of Natural Sciences in Philadelphia, and the Review of Natural History of London, just to name a few, were grateful to his contribution to the natural science. Richard Hill died on 28th September 1872.

Summary

Dr Richard Hill had a very interesting life one that could have taken many twists and turns, for example if he had been born to both a black mother and black father in Jamaica at that time its almost certain that he would have been enslaved. It's the author's belief that he still faced discrimination to a point. Hill was fortunate to receive a good education and even though his father was a white planter he inspired his son to go back to Jamaica and help his people and fight against the evil and inhumane institution of slavery which he did gladly, never forgetting the plight of his people.

References:

Great Jamaican Scientists Book 2, A.S. Johnson
The Legacy of Black Scientists & Inventors Vol 1, D-Ankh-Kheru

Mary Seacole

(1805-1881)

I was amazed and dumb-founded to hear how the former Minister for Education, Michael Gove MP, wanted to take Mary Seacole out of the British school curriculum. I understand that the pretext was that there is no relevance to British history. I believe that at the time of writing this, he has been unsuccessful with that initiative due to concerned groups protesting his decision.

One of the greatest contributions Jamaica has given to the world is the "Yellow Doctress", otherwise known as Mary Seacole. Mary Seacole was born in 1805, in Kingston, Jamaica. Her father was a Scottish army officer and her mother was a Jamaican of African descent who kept a boarding house principally for army officers. Growing up in the military, Seacole became fascinated with several aspects of army life such as travel and exploration. When Seacole was twelve, she was sent to England; when she returned to Jamaica, she became even more excited about travelling and had developed an interest in nursing.

In 1852, a cholera outbreak swept across the island of Jamaica. Seacole was of great service as she treated many of the sick with her own herbal remedies learned from her mother. Around the same time, she travelled to Panama where cholera was also raging and became invaluable there too.

In 1853, she returned to Jamaica where yellow fever was raging; again, she was of great service nursing the sick back to health by administering her remedies.

In 1854, England, France, and the Ottoman Empire (Turkey being at the centre) fought against Russia; this was known as the Crimean War. Seacole travelled to England offering her nursing services; however, she was refused because of her race and gender. Nevertheless, she continued to offer her services to the War Office and Florence Nightingale's own organisations, but each time she was met with an adamant "NO". Seacole, still determined, made her own way to the Crimea. Once there, she volunteered her services to various military hospitals and nursed the wounded and dying soldiers on the battlefield. The officers and men loved her and referred to her as "Mother Seacole"; soon enough, she was managing her own institution, which she called The British Hotel. The British Hotel served as a combination store, dispensary, and hospital for British officers.

Mary Seacole died in 1881 in England. She is buried in St. Mary's Catholic Cemetery in Kensal Rise, West London.

Sir William Howard Russell wrote of her, "I trust that England will not forget the one who nursed her sick and who sought out her wounded to aid and succour them and who performed the last office for some of her illustrious dead."

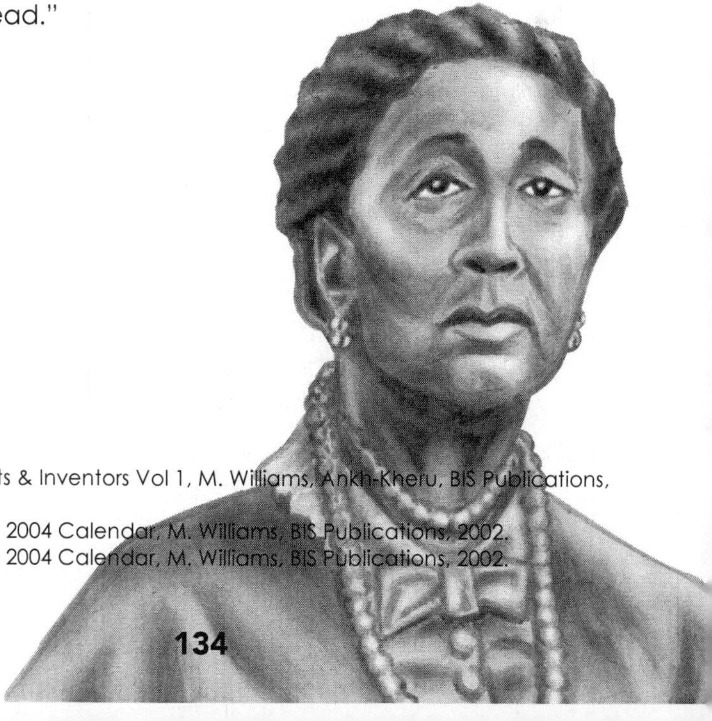

References:

Black Women Scientists & Inventors Vol 1, M. Williams, Ankh-Kheru, BIS Publications, 2007, 2010

Africa's Gift To Europe 2004 Calendar, M. Williams, BIS Publications, 2002.

Africa's Gift To Europe 2004 Calendar, M. Williams, BIS Publications, 2002.

Dr. James Africanus Beale Horton

(1835-1883)

James Beale Horton was born in the African country of Sierra Leone in 1835; his parents were once enslaved Africans of Igbo heritage. He was educated at the C.M.S (Church Missionary Society) in Freetown.

In 1855, at the request of the British War Office, Horton, along with William Davies and Samuel Campbell, who were also studying at the same institute, were chosen to further their medical training at King's College London. Horton studied at King's for three years and then attended a further year at the University of Edinburgh in order to earn an MD. Horton's thesis was entitled the Medical Topography of the West Coast of Africa. In 1859, he became the first African to graduate from the University of Edinburgh. Whilst at university, Horton renamed himself Africanus to demonstrate pride in his African heritage.

After completing his studies he went back to West Africa and entered the Army Service Corps as a staff assistant surgeon. During his time there he travelled to various posts across West Africa and was involved in both Ashanti wars of 1863 and 1873. Horton achieved the title Surgeon Major in 1874.

Whilst in West Africa, Horton became increasingly concerned with politics and political thought. Racial theories by European travelers at the time alleged the inferiority of Africans, which Horton actively contested in his books. For example, in 1868 his books entitled West African Countries and Peoples, British and Native and Vindication of the African Race dealt with the false propaganda.

In 1880, at just 45 years old, he retired and returned home where he founded the Commercial Bank of Sierra Leone, the first commercial bank in the region. His reason for establishing the bank was to help develop industries within Africa by funding local entrepreneurs and supporting infrastructure plans.

Horton spent the rest of his life committed to supporting African education by providing scholarships to promising young Africans. In 1883, Dr. James Africanus Beale Horton died at the age of 48 and at the time was deemed the wealthiest man in Africa. He left large parts of his wealth to the development of scientific education in Africa.

He is honoured by Edinburgh University as the first African to graduate, with a memorial plaque in Buccleuch Place, and a crater on Mercury is named after him.

Summary

Dr Africanus Horton had a very colourful life. Being born around the same year the Transatlantic Enslavement Trade ended he was fortunate to gain a scholarship to receive further and higher education. That said he must of have had to work hard to achieve it in the first place and also when he did receive the opportunity of extended education he did not waste it. Horton was proud of his heritage hence naming himself after the continent he was born in, but also challenged those who wrote negative propaganda about his people. Horton's life also shows us all that people of African descent have a long history of serving in the British arm forces, too often forgotten around remembrance days.

References:
We Were There, Directorate General Media and Communication, Ministry of Defence.

Dr. James Samuel Risien Russell

(1863-1939)

Risien Russell was lucky due to his parentage. His sugar planter father, William Russell, from the then region of Demerara (present day Guyana, South America), sent him and his brother William (born 1867) to the Dollar Academy in Scotland in 1880. He studied at Edinburgh University from 1882 to 1886, added a gold medal-winning M.D. in 1893 to his M.B. and C.M. from 1886, qualified for M.R.C.P. in 1891, then became a Fellow in 1897. Furthermore, he was awarded a B.M.A. scholarship in 1895, and studied in Berlin and Paris.

His first hospital appointment was in Nottingham; then he worked at the Brompton Tuberculosis Hospital and St. Thomas (London). He was a staff member of University College Hospital, then a professor from the 1890s when he was "the best known of the younger neurologists". Eight research articles by 1893 had doubled by 1908; he also contributed to reference works, notably on nervous disorders in Allbutt & Rolleston's System of Medicine. He was skilled at the diagnosis and management of diseases of the nervous system.

His private practice was at 44 Wimpole Street from the 1900s. He opened the neurological section of the B.M.A.'s July 1910 conference, speaking on epileptics. He was often a witness in legal cases involving lunacy, notably Harnett v. Bond (1924 - 5), and chaired the National Society for Lunacy Law Reform in the 1920s.

His house physician from 1923, Macdonald Critchley, recalled his "dark skin" and thought "he was one of the most important and

colourful figures within the medical profession of Great Britain" (The Ventricle of Memory, New York, 1990).

Having been the product of a mixed heritage marriage in Demerara (now Guyana) did not prevent James Risien Russell from achieving professional successes in Britain. He was a Captain in the Royal Army Medical Corps from 1908 to 1918; he was a professor at University College Hospital in the 1890s; he served on the management board of the Hospital for Nervous Diseases until 1928 and was an author of well-regarded articles in the medical press. His high-society private patients included explorer Sir Henry Stanley and best-selling novelist Mrs. Humphry Ward.

Risien Russell was a solid and respectable professional in London for four decades. He was described as "of mixed racial stock" with a private practice comprising, unusually, of "a large proportion of chronic psychotics and psycho-neurotics" (Queen Square and the National Hospital 1860 - 1960, 100-101). Queen Square includes a portrait photograph (also published in his obituary). The Highgate Cemetery memorial stone has Dr. J.S.R. Russell's name on the reverse and has William's name on the side. His brother had died suddenly and was recognised as a lawyer (KC - of the South African bar and had been based in Bulawayo (Rhodesia/Zimbabwe).

Dr. Risien Russell was not a stigmatised outsider but was part of English society. Russell is detailed in the Oxford Dictionary of National Biography September 2010; it already contains entries on Nelson and doctors Harold Moody, John Alcindor, and James Jackson Brown (also featured herein).

Dr. Risien Russell married Ada Gwenllian Michell in Kenwyn, Cornwall in July 1892; her father was a justice of the peace in Truro. Their daughter Marjory, or Marjorie, Gwenllian Russell was born in London 28 October 1893. In 1915, he was divorced by Ada, and in 1924, he married widow Ada Hartley who, with her son, Anthony, survived him.

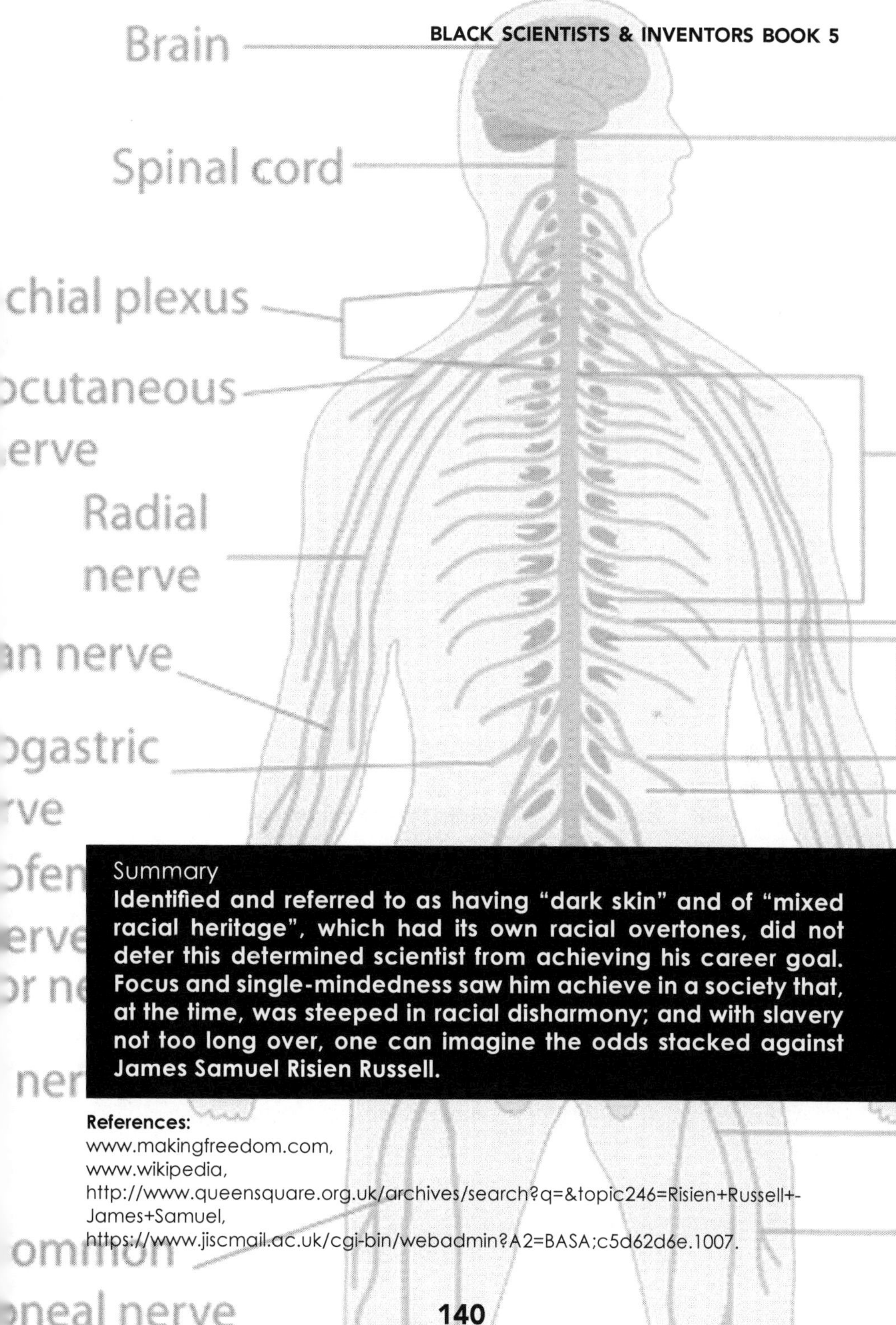

Summary

Identified and referred to as having "dark skin" and of "mixed racial heritage", which had its own racial overtones, did not deter this determined scientist from achieving his career goal. Focus and single-mindedness saw him achieve in a society that, at the time, was steeped in racial disharmony; and with slavery not too long over, one can imagine the odds stacked against James Samuel Risien Russell.

References:
www.makingfreedom.com,
www.wikipedia,
http://www.queensquare.org.uk/archives/search?q=&topic246=Risien+Russell+-James+Samuel,
https://www.jiscmail.ac.uk/cgi-bin/webadmin?A2=BASA;c5d62d6e.1007.

Dr. John Alcindor

(1873-1924)

Dr. John Alcindor was born on the Caribbean island of Trinidad & Tobago in 1873. He attended St. Mary's College in the Port of Spain, Trinidad. In 1893 he emigrated to Britain after winning a scholarship to study medicine at the University of Edinburgh (following in the footsteps of other great black scientists and inventors such as James Africanus Horton and Elijah McCoy). He successfully graduated in 1899 then moved to London where he worked in several hospitals including Hampstead, Plaistow, and Camberwell. In 1907, approximately eight years after arriving in London and working for others, he decided to set up his own practice in Acton before moving it to Paddington where he worked for 17 years. Whilst in London he mainly lived in West London, moving several times within that location.

Alcindor was a physician who also led research in areas such as cancer, influenza, and tuberculosis; his findings were published in medical journals. From 1917, Alcindor worked as Medical Officer of Health for the Paddington Poor Law Guardians. In 1919, during World War I, Alcindor, like most people of African descent who came from the British colonies, offered his service to be an officer in the Royal Army Medical Corp. Unfortunately, because he was of African descent, he was turned down as a colour bar was in place in England. But with similar determination as Mary Seacole and Harold Moody and as mentality of 'by any means necessary', Alcindor contributed to England's war efforts by working with the

Red Cross where he took care of the war casualties in London. He was awarded a medal for his services.

In 1900, Alcindor was involved in the first Pan-African Conference held in London. He also attended the Paris Pan-African Congress between 1919 and 1923. Along with John Archer, Alcindor was a founding member of the African Progress Union (APU), and in 1921, after Archer stepped down as chair, Alcindor took up the post. Alcindor must have been influenced by other Pan-Africanists like Henry Sylvester Williams and the Hon. Marcus Garvey, as he suggested that West Indians should move back to Africa and settle in countries like Uganda.

Dr. John Alcindor married Minnie Martin and they had three sons: Frank, Cyril, and Roland. His medical practice grew considerably amongst the poor, never turning away anyone who came for medical treatment, and he became known affectionately as the 'Black Doctor of Paddington'.

Dr. John Alcindor died on 25th October 1924, and is buried in St. Mary's Catholic Cemetery, Kensal Green, London.

Summary

Dr. Alcindor had a considerable practice among the poor of the Harrow Road neighbourhood, and was very popular among those who used to avail themselves of his medical skills and knowledge. He never allowed the obstacle of racism and prejudice to stop him from reaching for his goals. He also tried to make life better for other people of African descent who experienced racism in 1900s Britain.

References:

Naming And Role Model - highlighting African British Role Models 1907-2007, Kwaku, Published by BTWSC.
Making Freedom, A. Torrington, C. Dixon, 2013.
www.spartacus.schoolnet.co.uk?SLAalcindor.htm
www.blackpresence.co.uk.php

DR JOHN
ALCINDOR
1873 - 1924
SICIAN, PAN-AFRICANIS
D WWI LOCAL HERO
AD HIS SURGERY
ERE 1913-1924
NSTER COUNCIL
HARVIST TRUST

Dr. Harold Moody

"..If you are feeling inferior, make your self superior, and if you practice this all the time no one can attack what's in your mind..."

- Curtis Mayfield

Dr. Harold Moody

(1882-1947)

Dr. Harold Moody was born in Jamaica in 1882; his interest in science may have come from his father, who was a chemist. Moody emigrated to Britain in 1904 at the age of twenty-two in order to study medicine at King's College London. In 1910, Moody graduated and qualified as a medical doctor specializing in ophthalmics - medical and surgical eye problems.

Moody found it very difficult to get a job in his field due to the racial discrimination he experienced in England at that time. He recalled a hospital matron saying on record ''that she refused to have a coloured doctor working at the hospital". Even with doors closed to Moody, he did not allow that to deter him from practicing medicine. In 1913, he decided to construct his own 'Open Door' clinic, by setting up his own medical practice at 11 Kings Grove, Peckham, South East London. There were many doubters who thought he would fail, but his practice went on to be very successful.

Due to injustice and racial discrimination that people of African descent were facing in Britain at the time, and having experienced it first-hand, he decided to set up a black pressure group to fight for their rights and try to eliminate/challenge the colour bar. The group was called the 'League of Coloured People'. The group also provided welfare and social needs for many in the community. The 'League of Coloured People' also published its own magazine entitled The Key that showed the work the group was involved in. The great Caribbean Pan-Africanist and author of the Black Jacobins,

CLR James, was also a member of the 'League of Coloured People' and later became its chair.

During the 2nd World War, Moody tried to enlist to serve for Britain, but he was refused because of his colour. Determined to help in one way or another, he provided civil defense work as a doctor amongst the falling bombs in England.

Dr. Harold Moody died in 1947; his funeral in Camberwell was attended by thousands.

Summary

Dr. Harold Moody was born just 44 years after the Africans' emancipation from slavery in the Caribbean. Although it would have been a crime for his grandparents to learn how to read and write during slavery, Moody and his father took every opportunity afforded to free men to educate themselves. He took this onto another level by emigrating to England to further his education. Although facing discrimination and colour bars in England, he did not allow that to stop him from being all that God wanted him to be. He qualified as a medical doctor and because all doors were closed to him getting a job in that field, he set up his own practice. Due to discrimination he and his people faced in England, he set up a pressure group to help change the British culture of discrimination.

References:

Naming And Role Model - highlighting African British Role Models 1907-2007, Kwaku, Published by BTWSC.
The History Of The Black Presence In London
Making Freedom, A. Torrington, C. Dixon, 2013a
www.blacknet.co.uk/history/harold.html

Dr. James Jackson Brown of Hackney

(1882-1953)

James Jackson Brown was born in the St. Thomas district of Jamaica on 9 October 1882. His parents were considered well-off as they owned an estate and were able to afford to send him to Kingston private schools (York Castle and Jamaica College) and further on to Canada, where he started his medical studies. But Canadian education proved difficult, so halfway through his training, Brown decided to return to Jamaica. He then opted for England as his next destination. There he enrolled at the London Hospital on 22 September 1905.

After failing the second part twice, he eventually passed his examinations in October 1907. He then took on various jobs under renowned surgeons and physicians and worked for some time as a clinical clerk for Dr. Lord Dawson, who became King George V's physician. In 1911, he took part three, passing his examination in 1914.

As J. J. Brown, MRCS, LRCP, Dr. Brown started his medical practice in the east end of London. Brown was quite popular in his neighbourhood, especially after he established an all-black cricket team, the Africs, in the 1920s. Most of the cricketers on his team were fellow professionals such as lawyer Samuel Spencer Alfred in Cambridge (born in British Guiana) and Dr. John Alcindor in west London (born in Trinidad) (also featured in this publication). As they were not an established club with its own premises, they played away most times.

Dr. Brown's excellent reputation in the district was tarnished when he gave a local man a certificate that exempted him from military service. This saw Brown charged and struck off by the General Medical Council in early 1943, and he lost his right to practice medicine for issuing "an untrue certificate."

Brown died on 18 October 1953. His death was reported in the Hackney Gazette, and the heading read "Popular Hackney Doctor Dies". It also mentioned that he had been a "friendly, well-liked man with many interests, including Freemasonry. During the second world war he could only work at home for St. John Ambulance Brigade" as people of colour had difficulty getting recruited. This prejudice was more prevalent in the 1914 - 1918 war, as he was refused a commission in the Royal Army Medical Corps because he was black.

He dreamed of visiting Jamaica, telling people he was "a Maroon man", but he never went back.

The Africs, late 1920s. Brown (in cap) 3rd from left between Vivian Harris from St. Lucia or Antigua and G. R. Marcano (to Brown's left) from Trinidad who practiced in East Ham. Front left-right: Ivan Shirley, Roland Cumberbatch, and Ferdie Leekam – all doctors.

Summary

This is an earlier example of how difficult life was for 'people of colour'. But once again their resilience comes shining through and they even manage to have a little enjoyment on the way. Multi-facetted career means always moving forward, but more importantly helping others along the way. He serves as a fine example to us all.

References:

Jeffrey Green (historian) on wordPress.org - pg034

Dr. Alan Powell Goffe

(1920-1966)

Dr. Alan Powell Goffe was born in Kingston-Upon-Thames on 9th July 1920; his father was from Jamaica and his mother from England, both physicians. Life in England was difficult for all after the first world war, but more so for people of colour. The Goffe family avoided some of the prejudicial treatment but not entirely, as young Goffe was to find out.

Epsom College was known for its scientific leanings, and Goffe's early interest in science saw him enrolled in 1935 at 14 years old. However, these were the worst years of his life; the racism and bullying he was subjected to soon saw him sent away to complete his studies in Switzerland after only three years. Goffe applied and was accepted to study medicine at University College Hospital London in 1939.

During this time, two African Americans made news in the scientific world: Dr. Charles Richard Drew worked with blood storage leading later to his invention of the blood bank, and Dr. Percy Lavon Julian, a research chemist in the medicinal drugs arena, pioneered a treatment for glaucoma. This encouraged young black scientists everywhere, including Goffe.

Goffe's research study papers were well-received and also helped develop medicine that was put to public use in the 1950's. Two great things happened in the microbiology arena in the early 1950's. An American scientist, Dr. Jonas Salk, came up with a vaccine for poliomyelitis, a subject of interest to Goffe; and even more significant in 1953, was the discovery of DNA (deoxyribonucleic acid).

Some scientists were not too keen on Salk's injectable vaccine, their preference being oral administration, and Goffe was among this group. But 1955 saw Salk's success as the numbers of polio sufferers decreased dramatically.

Between 1955 and 1962, Salk was at the very top in his discipline, but Goffe helped fine tune the vaccine significantly reducing its side effects. Around the same time, American Dr. Albert Sabin created an oral vaccine and Goffe helped in its development and improvement, successfully excluding all side effects. Goffe also conducted pioneering work on what was called "the greatest killer of children in history", the measles virus. As a result of his contributions, a type of the measles virus was named after him -- "Goffe Strain". He was also one of the first scientists to conduct full-scale studies of the human wart virus, recently discovered as a cause of cervical cancer.

Dr. Alan Goffe married in 1943 and had four children. He died on August 13th, 1966, aged only 46, due to a sailing accident.

Summary

Once again we see the level of focus and purpose one has to maintain in order to achieve a chosen goal. The era that Dr. Goffe grew up in was a difficult one. WW1 was just over and the nation was heading towards WW2; the rise of fascism and other far right groups, with race riots and prejudice against people of colour, were on the increase. Not only did he graduate, but he also became politicised. He joined the then Labour Party and was one of the founding members of CND (Campaign for Nuclear Disarmament), joining protests all over Europe. Goffe's contributions are exemplary. His parents were very supportive and his middle-class upbringing helped shield him from more adverse racism. He is still one of the truly unsung heroes of our times.

References:

Between Two Worlds - The Story of Black British Scientist Goffe
(Gaia Goffe and Judith Goffe, MD – 2008).

Dr. Sir Arthur Wint

(1920-1992)

Arthur Stanley Wint OD, MBE was the first Jamaican Olympic gold medalist, winning the 400 m at the 1948 Summer Olympics.

Arthur Wint, known as the Gentle Giant, was born in Plowden, Manchester, Jamaica. While at Calabar High School, he ran sprints and did both high jump and long jump. He later transferred to Excelsior High School and finished his secondary education there. In 1937, he was the Jamaica Boy Athlete of the year; the following year he won a gold medal in the 800 m at the Central American Games in Panama.

In 1942, he joined the British Commonwealth Air Training Plan and set the Canadian 400 meter record while training there. He was sent to Britain for active combat during World War II as a pilot. He left the Royal Air Force in 1947 to attend St. Bartholomew's Hospital as a medical student. In 1953, he finished his internship, graduated as a doctor, and was made a Member of the British Empire (MBE) by Queen Elizabeth II the following year.

In 1948, Wint won Jamaica's first Olympic gold for the 400 meter (46.2) in London, beating his teammate Herb McKenley. He won silver in the 800 meter after American Mal Whitfield. He probably missed his third medal in the London games by pulling a muscle in the 4 x 400 meter relay final.

In Helsinki 1952, he was part of the historic team setting the world record while capturing the gold in the 4 x 400 meter relay. He also won silver in the 800 meter, again coming second to Mal Whitfield. He ran his final race in 1953 at Wembley Stadium.

In 1955, Wint returned to Jamaica eventually settling in Hanover as the only resident doctor in the parish. In 1973, he was awarded the Jamaica honour of the Order of Distinction. He served as Jamaica's High Commissioner to Britain and ambassador to Sweden and Denmark from 1974 to 1978. He was inducted in the Black Athlete's Hall of Fame in the US (1977), the Jamaica Sports Hall of Fame (1989), and the Central American & Caribbean Athletic Confederation Hall of Fame (2003).

Arthur Wint died on Heroes Day in Linstead, aged 72. He left behind an outstanding family as can be seen below and all have continued the legacy of excellence. A reviewer of his daughter's biography titled The Longer Run by Valerie Wint stated, "He was a father, husband, teammate and a friend but still managed to remain humble in spite of his professional success and personal trials." He is also considered the Jamaican father of sprints and is well-respected by the new and older sprinters who dominate the world stages in these disciplines. Before Usain Bolt there was Dr. Arthur Wint OD, MBE.

Summary

Multi-faceted nature of life is evident here again at all levels and not only did Arthur Wint study and graduate in his chosen profession of medicine, but at the same time engaged in sports at international level; was a pilot during the second world war, and later served as a diplomat in the roles of high commissioner (London) and ambassador (Sweden & Denmark) for his country of birth, Jamaica. The focus and determination needed to achieve such levels only goes to show that against all odds dreams can be achieved if you want them strongly enough. He was, indeed, an exemplary figure.

References:

The Gleaner, Jamaica 30/11/2011 | 'The longer run' - A daughters story of Arthur Wint-, biography by Valerie Wint (Dr.) 20/09/2011. | Wikipedia | YouTube | Valiant Women: Profiles of African Women In Struggle 1500s to 1970s, Zindika Kamauesi, BIS Publications, 2010

Professor Charles Ssali

(1930-2004)

Professor Charles Ssali was an African doctor and inventor born in 1930, in Masaka, Uganda. Ssali attended St. Henry's College, Kitovu, Uganda where he passed his Cambridge school certificate with five distinctions and four credits -- the highest pass in East African schools for 1953. He then went on to Makerere University Kampala, where he passed the higher school certificate (A's) in 1955. He continued with pre-clinical training in anatomy and physiology for two years followed by clinical years in medicine and surgery leading to the degree of MBCHB in 1960.

During 1960 to 1962, Ssali worked in several hospitals in Uganda; he completed an internship with Mulago Hospital from January to December 1961 and began work in general medical practice from 1962. He worked at Entebbe Hospital for six months followed by one year in Bombo Hospital where he was in charge of medical and surgical problems including obstetrical and gynecological patients.

He came to the UK in 1964 to continue his studies at Royal College of Surgeons in Lincoln's Inn Fields, gaining primary FRSC. He continued to specialise and practice in Ear Nose and Throat (ENT) at Scotland at Royal College of Surgeons and also became a registrar at the Victoria Hospital in Fife.

Later, Ssali worked at the Royal Infirmary in Edinburgh as a registrar as part of his training. He passed the final examination of Fellow of the Royal College of Surgeons in April 1967 -- the highest examination degree in medicine and surgery.

He later managed to return to Uganda as a registrar and continued to work and research in his specialized field (ENT) in his home country as well as the neighbouring countries like Kenya. There he was a consultant surgeon at the National Hospital from 1974 - 1984 before returning to the UK for further research and back as a consultant to various hospitals in and around southeast UK and Scotland.

In the meantime, whilst in the UK, he was carrying out his own private research to develop a treatment for HIV/AIDS. In 1992, he invented a treatment for the disease/virus called "Mariandina A, B and J", for which he received a British patent. The treatment involves taking a course of 100% natural food supplement tablets fortified with powerful antioxidants, natural vitamins, and 29 herbs such as ginseng and garlic. All of these ingredients are rare elements used to cleanse, rejuvenate, and build a strong healthy body. Mariandina works by providing cells in the body with vitamins and anti-oxidants that cleanse our body of free radicals. Free radicals in the body are what rust is to metal; they damage the cells and assist in the reproduction of viruses.

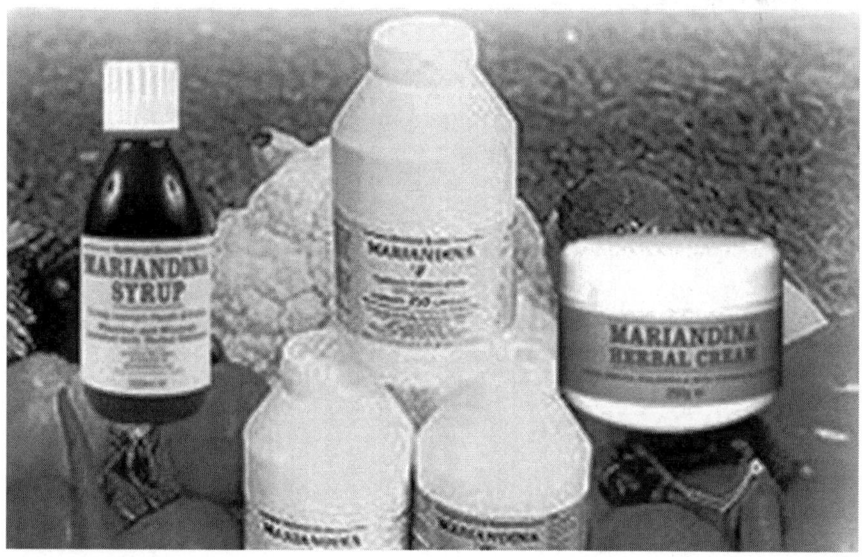

Mariandina allows the cells to function correctly and builds a healthy immune system. Professor Ssali's invention treats illnesses such as asthma, lupus, arthritis, kidney disease, various forms of cancer, diabetes, sickle cell, and eczema. Mariandina can also help those who have suffered from a stroke.

Professor Ssali has added to his list of inventions, treatments for diseases such as atrophic rhinitis (Kibobe); rhino scleroma, and laryngo tracheobronchitis. Using Mariandina, Prof. Ssali has had an 80% success rate for treating patients with HIV/AIDS. Professor Ssali was a director of the Mariandina Aids Research Foundation and has been hailed a national hero by the Ugandan people.

Professor Charles Ssali died in March 2004; his son, Stephen Ssali, a qualified electronic engineer, has now taken on the Mariandina Aids Research Foundation project and is very successful at continuing his fathers work.

Summary

Those born to fulfill a purpose in life can not be summarised. Dr. Ssali's country had not achieved independence when he qualified as a doctor; one can only imagine the manner of obstacles he had to surmount in order to reach the highest echelons of the profession. It seems he was hell bent on reaching the final goal; as if on a mission to accomplish and did exactly that with a natural flare in a very short space of time before he himself had to transcend. The legacy left behind is a formidable one.

References:

Black Scientists & Inventors 1999 Calendar, BIS Publications, 1998.

Black Scientists & Inventors Book 3, M. Williams, BIS Publications, 2007.

Ron Headley

(1939)

Ron was born in Kingston, Jamaica in 1939; he emigrated from Jamaica to Birmingham, England with his parents in 1952. Ron is known for his simple but effective ideas. In 1985, he invented a "cleaner diesel engine emission system" he called the Eco-Charger.

The Eco-Charger improves the performance of diesel cars by reducing smoke emission and fuel consumption and allowing cars to run for 150,000 miles without major maintenance. Ron's innovation succeeds where others fail. Ron explains, "It works on the fuel before combustion, so there is no need for a Catalytic Converter to clean up the exhaust afterwards ... It's like a 'mini refinery under the car bonnet.'" Ron set up a company in Birmingham that currently manufactures the Eco-Charger.

In 1998, it was reported in national UK newspapers that Ron Headley had a meeting with representatives of a major automobile company and was offered 6 million pounds for his Eco-Charger. Ron declined the offer and chose to market and sell the Eco-Charger through his own company. He received support from many people including his friends, ex-West Indies cricket captain Clive Lloyd and ex-footballer Cyrille Regis.

The Eco-Charger improves our environment and allows us all to breathe cleaner air. Ron Headley is not just an innovator/inventor who has several patents to his name. He also comes from a rich background of great cricket players. From 1958 to 1974 he played cricket for Worcestershire and internationally for the West Indies in 1973. His father, George Headley, also played for the West Indies, and Ron Headley's son, Dean Headley, played international cricket for England during the 1990s.

Summary

Ron Headley is one of those people who can't be compartmentalized, he has shown this throughout his life. As a man coming from a long legacy of cricketers, Ron could have rested on his fathers laurels or just followed in his footsteps which he did but Ron had even more ambitious plans up his sleeves. He had the audacity to invent a motor engine part that would compete at the highest level in the motor industry. His invention made motor engines more efficient, environmentally friendly which lead to cleaner air.

References:

Black Scientists & Inventors Book 1, M. Williams, A. Henry. BIS Publications, 1999, 2003, 05, 07. Simply The Best, A.A.D. , M. Williams, BIS Publications, 2010

Dr. Geoff (Godfrey) Palmer

(1940)

Professor Godfrey Henry Oliver Palmer was born in St. Elizabeth, Jamaica in 1940. He grew up in Kingston, Allman Town. He loved soccer and cricket, he developed the latter to a very competent level on the Race course fields [now called National Heroes Park]. This love of cricket was to elevate him and prove a foundation and a ticket in his later years. In Jamaica he played for the Kingston Senior School cricket team.

Just short of his 15th birthday in 1955, Godfrey's mother, who had travelled to London, England a few years before, sent for him.

When he arrived in London, his mother looked for work for him, to replace the £80.00 she spent for his aeroplane ticket. But because of his age, it was illegal for him to work full-time, so he had to attend school. At Shelbourne Road Secondary Modern at Nags Head, Holloway, newly arrived Palmer was given a customary IQ test, and due to the language and cultural differences, he was classified as educationally sub-normal (ESN). He also discovered that he was the only black person in the school.

His athleticism, especially in cricket, soon saw him selected as the only boy ever from a secondary modern school to play for London School Boys Cricket Team (the Islington Gazette even published a picture of him). This, in turn, led to a requested transfer from the headmaster of Highbury County Grammar school where he was placed in the educational "slow stream".

Once again, despite this, Palmer left school three years later with three O-levels and one A-level.

In 1958, he applied and gained employment as a junior lab technician at Queen Elizabeth College, London working for Professor Garth Chapman, after seeing an advertisement in the papers. Between 1958 and 1961, Palmer obtained two further 'A' levels and had a full grant awarded, but again acceptance at university proved difficult. (By this time he had attained a total of four A-levels and eight O-levels.) Professor Chapman, however, managed to get Palmer admitted at Leicester University in 1961, and by 1964, Palmer had his degree in botany.

After his studies and back in London, Palmer found that the job market was not so welcoming, even with his qualifications, so he got a job as a potato peeler to try and make ends meet. Today he jokes about this as the only job he could get close to his degree in botany.

Although Palmer was turned down to study a master's degree, he was accepted to study for a joint doctorate degree in grain science and technology at Herriot-Watt College and Edinburgh University. He began his doctorate in 1965 and finished it in fewer than three years. In 1968, he began research work at the Brewing Research Foundation in Surrey as a grain scientist, specialising in barley and introducing the abrasion process, which revolutionised the international brewing industry. In 1977, he left this position as a senior scientist and returned to Scotland to work as a lecturer at Herriot-Watt College. He helped graduate students from all over the world in grain technology until his retirement. His awards are numerous and Palmer became one of, if not the foremost, grain specialist in the world.

Palmer somehow also found time to help members of his community with reading and writing skills, plus a little advocacy as well. He is still involved, similarly, even after his retirement.

Summary

Dr. Palmer's career is exemplary in focus and tenacity, against all adversity. Despite hurdles strewn along his educational path, including racist discrimination and prejudice as demeaning work for one so highly qualified, he forged on and achieved his goal to such high levels that he stands as a beacon to all races. His achievements received the highest awards and recognitions.

- **1998 American Society of Brewing Chemists Award (first European scientist recipient) (fourth ever at the time)**
- **2002 William Darling Good Citizens Award (community race relations)**
- **2003 OBE**
- **2004 Black Enterprise UK Champion**
- **2011 Freeman of Midlothian, an award he shares with such greats as Nelson Mandela**

Emeritus Professor Geoff Palmer still found time to champion race relations and mentor young African Caribbean children in maneuvering the education system in the UK.

As we prepare to publish, we learned that Professor Geoff Palmer has just been nominated onto the 2014 Queens New Year's Honours list, to receive a Knight Bachelor Award for services to science, human rights, and charity.

On this, in an interview in the London Jamaican Times of January 2014, Prof. Palmer says, "I am quite happy that the award is partly for the work in my professional life because many times when members of our community are recognised it is for community work. And while that is great, I am happy to be recognised for the work that I did, that has made a difference internationally. *"Arise Professor Emeritus, Sir Geoff Palmer!*

On education in the same interview, he states, "I realise that we can go nowhere without education. We all need to work to get better educational opportunities for our young people who are deprived. Education gives you the opportunity to become more mobile. Without education you're stuck. Education gives you choices."

On parents, Palmer says,

"I am saying to the kids today, don't underestimate your parents. If they're doing the best for you, do the best for them. Sometimes you may feel that it is not enough but be aware that sometimes they are giving all that they have got and that should be enough."

References:
www.catchavibe.co.uk , www.historicalgeographies.blogspot.co.uk, www.100greatblackbritons.com, The Jamaican Times newspaper, 2014

"...Life is one big road with lots of signs, so when your riding through the ruts don't complete your mind... Don't bury your thoughts; put your vision to reality..."

- Robert Nester Marley

Professor Sir Bernard Ribeiro

Professor Sir Bernard Ribeiro

(1944)

Bernard Ribeiro was born in 1944, in Achimota, Ghana. Ribeiro moved to the UK with his family at the age of eight. He attended Dean Close School in Cheltenham. He then attended London University's Middlesex Hospital Medical School. At that medical school he qualified as a medical doctor in 1967.

In 1972, he was awarded the Fellowship of the Royal College of Surgeons of England (FRCS). According to the online encyclopedia Wikipedia, the FRCS is a professional qualification to practice as a senior surgeon in Ireland or the United Kingdom. It is bestowed by the Royal College of Surgeons of England, Royal College of Surgeons in Ireland (chartered 1784), Royal College of Surgeons of Edinburgh (chartered 1505), and Royal College of Physicians and Surgeons of Glasgow, though strictly the unqualified initials refer to the London College.

At Basildon Hospital in 1979, Ribeiro was appointed consultant general surgeon, which meant that he was reaching the top of his career. He had a special interest in urology and colorectal surgery. But Ribeiro's major contribution to British society, and in fact the world, came in 1991 when he introduced keyhole surgery at Basildon Hospital.

In 1998, he was elected to the Council of the Royal College of Surgeons of England. Ribeiro had significant influence in the awarding of university status for both Basildon and Thurrock hospitals in 2002. He also helped to establish the Basildon and Thurrock

University Hospitals NHS Foundation Trust's advanced laparoscopic unit. Outside of the UK, Ribeiro has also worked as a consultant surgeon in Ghana and as an examiner in surgery at three universities.

In 2004, Ribeiro was awarded the CBE for his services to medicine; just four years later, he was knighted.

Professor Sir Ribeiro retired from medical service in 2008, but not before receiving, in that same year, an honorary degree of Doctor of Science by Anglia Ruskin University and an honorary doctorate fellowship, from the American College of Surgeons.

As well as carrying out his duties as a peer where he was raised in 2010, Baron Ribeiro also acts as one of the advisers to the Secretary of State for Health.

Summary

Sir Barnard Ribeiro came from humble beginnings in Ghana, but when he came to the UK he took advantage of the education system in order to get as much out of it as possible which resulted in him becoming a medical doctor. But from his story we can see that he has been giving back as much and even more to British society than what he took out. Ribeiro demonstrates that with ambition and drive a person can get to the top of any profession regardless of their beginnings.

References:

http://en.m.wikipedia.org/wiki/Bernard_Ribeiro,_Baron_Ribeiro
The Naming And Role Model Project 2010.

Dr. Tim C.P. Tavares

(1950s circa)

Dr. Tim Tavares was born on the Caribbean island of Jamaica in the 1950s where he attended school until he emigrated with his family to England, first to the Midlands but finally settling in London. Tavares completed a chemistry degree at London University, attaining first class honours. He also completed a PhD in material science and electronics with sensors at Imperial College London.

He has worked as both an engineer and professor in a number of countries around the world such as Greece and South Africa.

cessing

Tavares is also an entrepreneur; he set up a company called Basis Volume, which was involved in advanced materials research and development during the 1980s. At that time, Basis Volume had a 6-year-lead on any other company working with superconductor technology. Tavares and his staff at Basis Volume have made significant contributions to areas of solid-state science, in particular high-temperature conductors, superconductivity, fuel-cell, and solid state chemical sensor developments. The high-temperature superconductors are used in instruments such as medical scanners, high power motors, magnetic separators, and very high-speed tunnel trains.

Tavares' pioneering work -- the world's-first-high TC Super Conducting Tube -- was on display at the famous London Science Museum during the late 1980s. Tavares has also presented to young people the topic of superconductivity and black inventors in general. He has also appeared on Michael Williams' "Black Scientists & Inventors" program. Dr. Tim Tavares is also involved in open source technologies, network computers, and network analogue instrumentation. He passionately develops, teaches, and promotes the benefits of using open source software. He created the first South London Linux users group, B-Lux.

Summary

Dr. Tim Tavares' pioneering work has allowed him to invent products that have revolutionized electronic chemical sensor products and the industry in general. His work has allowed instruments such as medical scanners to be made much more affordable for hospitals. Dr. Tavares' work has been directly and indirectly incorporated in devices that use superconductor technology in the UK and around the world, thereby providing a huge service to humanity.

References:

Our Story: A Handbook of African History and Contemporary Issues, Edited by Akyaaba Addai-Sebo and Ansel Wong, Published by London Strategic Policy Unit 1988.

KJ Academy 2005 Calendar, K. Rickard, KJ Academy, Published 2004.

www.blug.org

Pauline Straker-Rodgers

(1950)

Pauline Straker-Rodgers was born in 1950 in Kingston, Jamaica to Granville and Ann Clarke Straker. She attended Greenwich Primary School in Whitfield town. Straker-Rodgers became interested in making dolls as a hobby, which was encouraged by both her mother and neighbour.

After Straker-Rodgers settled in the UK, she attended the Ellen Beddington's doll-making classes in Beckenham. It was at this time she decided she wanted to pursue doll-making as a career. Whilst fine-tuning her skills, she realized that a doll's clothes, hairstyle, and other characteristics can be used to depict its cultural heritage. She saw this evidence in European and, to some extent, Chinese dolls, whilst dolls of African descent had been mere caricatures.

Straker-Rodgers believes that dolls reflect a person's cultural heritage and give a sense of identity and pride. For this reason she is careful to get the design of the clothes and features of the doll correct. Straker-Rodgers states with this in mind and encouragement from family and friends, she decided to start making her own African wigs and costumes. Friends were impressed with her designs and asked her to host a number of seminars to teach these skills.

In 1997, Straker-Rodgers came to international attention when she was invited by the Global Doll Society (GDS) to become one of its specialty teachers. This made her the only recognised teacher in the world of African wigs and costumes. At the 1998 GDS convention, Straker-Rodgers, along with her 10-year old daughter, won prizes for their doll costumes. Pauline has also won the Dollcrafter Excellence Award at the ARAL Doll Festival in 2008 and the Butternut challenge at the Dollmakers Circle.

Pauline Straker-Rodgers continues creating dolls, winning competitions, and conducting seminars and leading workshops in the UK and Europe.

Summary

Pauline Straker-Rodgers uses her specialized doll making skills to depict images of people from her own culture; in the same way that the The Most Honourable Marcus Garvey saw value of African children being exposed to dolls which looked them. She has also used this rare but very much needed craft to teach her country folk the art of doll making. Pauline says: *"I want to use my dolls to portray positive images of people's culture."*

References:

Black Scientists & Inventors Book 2, M. Williams, BIS Publications, 2003, 05, 07.

Jerry Yamoa

(1950-2008)

Jerry Yamoa was born in the Asante region of Ghana on 7th July 1950, to Mrs. Comfort Adwoa Adoma and Mr. Nana Kyei Mensah. Jerry was very close to his grandmother, Akua Asirifia, who lived in Agogo. She took responsibility for his upbringing from childhood. Akua often took the young Yamoa to the bush in search of her secret herbal cures taken from leaves, roots, and tree bark so that he could learn by observing her. Jerry was fascinated with his grandmother's vast knowledge of plants and her ability to distinguish between various medicinal shrubs. Jerry remembered people who lived in and around Agogo visiting his house for treatment for respiratory complaints.

Akua's treatment was also used in the 1940s and 1950s for people suffering from tuberculosis, which is an infectious wasting disease that affects the lungs.

The chief medical officer of the local hospital was so convinced about its properties, he tried it out on asthma sufferers who went to the hospital for treatment. To his amazement it quickly alleviated their suffering. This doctor, amongst others, tried to coerce the secret from Akua, but she did not tell. In 1994, Akua finally passed her secret on to her grandson Jerry just before she died at 107 years of age.

Jerry was aware that there were millions of people around the world suffering from respiratory complaints such as asthma, bronchitis, sinusitis, and hay fever. He vowed that the world must not be denied this extraordinary product, which now markets as Yamoa Powder™. In the United Kingdom, alone, well over 5000 people have taken this food supplement with a success rate of 90%. Yamoa Powder™ is a 100% natural food supplement that is taken over a four-week course. Within one week, a person suffering from asthma, hay fever, and other respiratory complaints should notice significant improvements. It can be taken by both adults and children.

Jerry Yamoa was also a qualified primary school teacher and taught in Accra, Ghana. He also studied journalism whilst living in the UK.

Summary

As we researched and at times coming across some of the most highly qualified, innovative and outstanding scientist, equally you come across the likes of Jerry Yamoa and his almost magical powder you wonder if we are truly headed in the right direction. A teacher with ingenuity that has managed to bring traditional medicine, passed on to him by his grandmother, to the modern market. It takes a very special mind to achieve this.

References:

Black Scientists & Inventors Book 2, M. Williams, BIS Publications, 2003, 05, 07.

Leeroy Brown

(1959)

Leeroy Brown was born in August 1959 in London. His parents, Leeland and Sylvette Brown, emigrated from St. Thomas in Jamaica in 1954, initially settling in London before moving to Birmingham. Brown grew up with his six siblings.

Brown attended both Adderley Road Infant and Primary School and then Mirfield Secondary School. He was an average student but loved math, woodwork, technical drawing, and P.E. He finished there in 1974 and then went to Tamworth College, taking an engineering course in mechanics, whilst working as an apprentice/trainee mechanic.

Brown's fascination with inventions came as a young adult at the age of 25. He recalls "...when I had my first idea which I did nothing about. This idea later materialised via someone else. Hence my going the full length with this innovation."

Brown's first invention was an accelerator, brake and clutch locking device, - across all three pedals.

In September 2002, Leeroy Brown developed an innovative combination air pump and car jack in conjunction with engineers from Sheffield Hallam University. For this invention, he filed a UK patent in 2000 and won a major national award. Leeroy Brown beat stiff competition to win the Consumer Award and a £5000 prize at the BBC's Tomorrow's World Awards, in association with NESTA.

Inventor Leeroy Brown came up with his invention after a long road trip. "I kept seeing people struggling to change their tyres at the side of the road and I thought there's got to be an easier way," says the inventor. After studying the emergency services, he found that they used air-bags to lift vehicles, and this gave him an idea.

Brown set about putting his vision and ideas down on paper, and when he was happy with what he had, he started to build models of his sketches. When he had taken his design and development as far as he could, he embarked upon getting some financial and technical help. He approached Sheffield Hallam University's engineering department for help with the development of the concept. The engineers liked the idea and decided to team up with him.

Brown's invention is powered by a car battery and works when it is plugged into the car's cigarette lighter socket; it uses a compressor to inflate a rubber air-bag, which raises the car safely and easily. It also has another function; if another pipe is fitted to the device, it can be used to inflate tyres.

Brown was awarded a further £38,500 grant from NESTA, which helped him pay for a new design that can fit inside of any car.

Stuart Scholey, a design engineer of the University's SCEPTRE said "It's great to see Leeroy's idea getting the attention it clearly deserves after the time and effort he has put into the project."

Leeroy Brown hopes that his invention will end the misery for motorists who have to grapple with a traditional car jack when they get a flat tyre.

The road for many inventors is often a hard and lonely one. Even when inventors think they have made major progress, setbacks and heartache can be just around the corner. Brown has gone through many of these over the years, even before and after winning the BBC's Best Inventors award.

But Brown has an unstoppable will. He is self-determined and his sense of define purpose is unwavering; to this end he continues to invest his time and much of his own money including putting his home up as collateral.

Leeroy Brown continues to develop the car jack combination and has made major improvements. His latest version is good to go to the manufacturing stage and just needs additional capital investment and publicity.

Summary

If one ever needed to learn first hand what a definite purpose is, persistence, steadfastness and a will to win, then you only need to study the lives of most inventors and in this case you don't need to go any further than Leeroy Brown to see these qualities in practice. Brown has put everything in his life on the line to achieve his goal, he is proof that when one becomes successful it's not due to some sort of luck bestowed upon them at birth, but through had work and persistence luck is created.

References:
Black Scientists & Inventors Book 3, M. Williams.
BBC's Best Inventor.

Leeroy Brown

Dr. Elizabeth Rasekola

(1960)

Elizabeth Rasekoala was born on 17 May 1960, in Lagos, Nigeria. As a child, Dr. Rasekoala was interested in math and chemistry. In 1983, she attended Ahmadu Bello University where she obtained a bachelor's degree in chemical engineering. Dr. Rasekoala continued her education by travelling to the UK where she gained a master's degree in chemical engineering in 1986 at the University of Manchester.

Dr. Rasekoala has now worked in the chemical engineering industry for over twenty years in both Nigeria and the UK. She focuses much of her energy on education, being involved in the schooling of African Caribbean students, particularly in the areas of math, science, and technology. Dr. Rasekoala found that many black students in the UK were under-achieving in these subjects; subsequently, she started the UK-based African Caribbean Network for Science and Technology. She also initiated the Ishango Science Club and RESPECT campaign. Dr. Rasekoala has written about the scientific achievements of black students in local and national press as well as in academic journals.

She has been a keynote speaker in the USA, Canada, South Africa, and many European countries. She is a member of Business in the Community: Opportunity 2000 - National Focus on Women panel; Qualifications and Curriculum Authority (QCA) - Advisory Group on Race; and many other professional societies in the chemical engineering field.

In January 1991, Dr. Elizabeth Rasekoala received a commendation from the Commonwealth Association of Science, Technology, and Mathematics Educators (C.A.S.T.M.E) for innovation in recognition of her work in conceptualising and developing the *Ishango Science Club in the UK.

The African Caribbean Network for Science is a national educational charity, established in 1995 by black professionals working in various fields of science, engineering, and technology. The purpose of the organisation is to advance the educational achievements and career aspirations of black youth in these areas where they are very much under-represented due to inequalities of the mainstream educational system within the U.K.

Extra Notes: *The Ishango bone dates back to 20,000 BC. It was found in Rutanzige a small African village bordering Zaire and Uganda. It is the oldest instrument found to date which was used for advance mathematics. The oldest instrument for basic mathematics & measurements is the Lebombo bone, which was found in the Lebombo mountain region in Swaziland.

Summary

Although Dr. Elizabeth Rasekoala has become very successful in her area of science, she has shown a selfless attitude towards others. She wants others to also benefit from the rewards of a successful career in science. Her extra curricular activities are helping hundreds and thousands of children in the UK realise their dreams.

References:
Black Scientists & Inventors Book 3, M. Williams.

Peter Sesay

(1961-2009)

Peter Sesay was born 6th June 1961 in Shepherds Bush, London, England to a father from Sierra Leone and mother from England. Peter Sesay attended Isaac Newton Secondary School in West London. An average student, Peter gained eight CSEs. His favourite subjects were PE, metalwork, woodwork, art, and English. Since he was more practical than academic, Sesay did particularly well in art, metalwork, and technical drawing, achieving CSE grades 1 and 2 in these subjects.

Sesay always knew he wanted a career in engineering and research and development. Sesay became the man of the house at the age of ten when his father died, and from the age of eleven, Sesay would fix appliances and furniture around the house for his mother.

After completing his secondary education, Sesay went straight into an engineering apprenticeship with the company Hoover Ltd.

Sesay has been working in the field of engineering since the age of 16. During that time he has developed a number of skills which include mechanical engineering, product design, research and development, and leadership. In 1987, Sesay started his own business whilst working full time for United Biscuits.

He ran his company for over 20 years, during that time Sesay noticed that many customers had complaints about car seat belts. The problem was that regular car seat belts cut across the necks of children, which made them very uncomfortable. Sesay discovered that, although there were many complaints, there were no solutions to the problem. So he set to work on developing a device that could solve the problem in a simple, user-friendly, and safe way. After successful completion, Peter Sesay received a UK and European patent for the device that he developed.

In 2005, he set up a company named Autosafe Products of which he owns 50%. The other 50% belongs to Duncan Bannatyne and Peter Jones, angel investors from the hit BBC series Dragons Den. In the deal made on the BBC programme, Sesay received a £100,000 investment to release the 50% share to the dragons. Both Duncan Bannatyne and Peter Jones helped Sesay in the areas of public relations and advertising. Peter Jones said that Peter Sesay's invention was "the best he had seen in the entire series of the Dragon's Den."

In his book Riding the Storm, Duncan Bannatyne writes "Auto Safe was a seat-belt adapter that made seat belts much safer for children to use; it had been invented by a lovely man called Peter Sesay... If it saves even one child's life it would be the best investment we ever made."

Sadly, soon after Peter Sesay received the investment, he died of cancer. Before Peter Sesay passed, he said to me (co-author of this book) that he would like to inspire children to believe in and try to achieve their dreams.

Summary

Peter Sesay showed us that you should never give up on your dreams. His story also illustrates that you don't have to come from a wealthy family or even attend the best schools to be a great achiever. Instead all that is needed is drive, ambition and a desire to achieve your goals. He had achieved just that with his inventions and in particular his Car Seat Belt Adjuster invention. Before Peter Sesay died he left us all truly one of Gods blessings an invention that would save countless lives in car accidents all over the world.

References:

Black Scientists & Inventors Book 3, M. Williams.

BBC's Dragon's Den

Ron Headley

"simplicity is the key to all good inventions"

- Ron Headley

Dr. Donald Palmer

(1962)

"We are already seeing that many of the jobs require a STEM-based knowledge; therefore, it is important that our black British children have an appreciation of this subject area."

Gadman and Irene Palmer arrived in England from Clarendon, Jamaica, in the 1960s with their three young children. They were among many West Indians who travelled from Caribbean countries to the UK during the 1950s and 1960s. British politicians such as Enoch Powell visited their countries in a recruitment effort for the United Kingdom to help rebuild the country since some of its infrastructure was damaged due to bombing during WWII. So there was plenty of work but not enough labour. Gadman worked on the buses, and Irene worked as an auxiliary nurse for the National Health Service.

In 1962, Palmer was born in Tooting, South London. He attended Ernest Bevin Secondary School where he completed his Certificate of Standard Education (C.S.E) achieving Grade 1, the highest grade. It must be said that this is a great achievement as many Caribbean children in the UK during the 1960s and 70s were automatically placed in Educational Subnormal Units (ESN), whether they were academically capable or not. Palmer remembers that his parents had an immense influence on his academic career: "They encouraged me to work hard. At Christmas when I was a teenager they bought me a chemistry set which was the start of my love affair with science. And I'll never forget what my father told me - 'Every generation must rise not fall.'"

Palmer's favorite subjects at school were chemistry, biology, and physics. He was fascinated with understanding how the body works and he also enjoyed reading science-fiction books and spent hours reading Marvel comics. He also remembers being inspired by his chemistry teacher Mr. Irving. "He made chemistry exciting and I looked forward to his lessons. I also won a prize, which was a chemistry book that I still have to this day."

After leaving Ernest Bevin in 1981, Palmer attended South London College and attained an Ordinary National Diploma (OND) in medical science. He continued his studies by taking medical science at Bradford University where he earned a BSc (Hons) in 1985. He then attended King's College to study immunology; there he received his master's in 1988. Palmer was not satisfied with that as he had not yet reached his goal; he therefore continued his studies whilst developing his practical skills by working at the Northwick Park Hospital MRC Clinic Sciences Centre. In 1992, Palmer received his PhD for his thesis titled 'Investigating the Genetic Regulation of Beta-2 Microglobulin'.

To date, Dr. Donald Palmer now has his own research lab, has had many scientific papers published, and has been invited to give presentations all around the world. He holds the position of Senior Lecturer in Immunology at the Royal Veterinary College and is a Senior Honorary Lecturer at Imperial College London. In the 2000s, Dr. Donald Palmer received a UK Patent for an anti-cancer reagent.

When asked if there is a glass ceiling in science for black scientists, inventors, and entrepreneurs, Palmer replies, "Not necessarily, things are hard but it's about having desire and building your network."

Dr. Donald Palmer has participated in Michael Williams' Black Scientists & Inventors program. He relaxes by jogging and occasionally writes for an online Jazz magazine (Vibe-UK).

Dr. Donald Palmer

Summary

Palmer's message to black children in particular and all children in general is that science underpins everything we do and will continue to do so. The advancements made in medicine, communication, and computing clearly illustrate this. Moreover, the solutions for this planet will require expertise in STEM subjects. Therefore, it is imperative that young people embrace the subjects and make a contribution to solving the challenges ahead.

References:

Interview with Donald Palmer.

Dr. Yvonne Greenstreet

(1963)

Dr. Yvonne Greenstreet was born in Ghana in 1963. She is the senior vice-president of medicine development and speciality care at Pfizer. Greenstreet's career has involved the development of important new drugs for GlaxoSmithKline (GSK) and currently at Pfizer.

At GSK, where she spent the first 18 years of her career in the industry, she worked on important new drugs such as Zofran, for preventing chemo-associated nausea and vomiting, and also Valtrex that is used against genital herpes. The list is endless and all were mega deals.

Greenstreet decided to leave the practice of medicine to pursue an MBA (INSEAD Fontainebleau in France). This was a hard decision to make and follow as there were strong objections from colleagues, friends, and even family. Greenstreet is quoted as having said to these objections, "But it's what I wanted to do, so I did it. I think it was a really important experience for me that has been quite formative for me in my career. As I said, take on different opportunities. Have courage to follow what you believe is important."

At Pfizer, she's one of the senior research and development leaders bringing new treatments to patients through its speciality care unit. This unit has been and continues to be responsible for drugs and treatments such as

- Tofacitinib, which the Food & Drug Association (FDA) has

approved for treating rheumatoid arthritis

- The development of other drugs to combat cancer, autoimmune conditions, and infectious diseases
- In 2012, her group continued refining its meningitis B vaccine
- Prevnar 13, which is a anti-pneumonia vaccine.

In the human health area, Pfizer partner GlycoMimetics has made great advances for patients with sickle cell disease, which is prevalent in people of African, Asian, and South European descent; this is an area of interest for Greenstreet.

Her own experiences in West Africa influenced her desire to treat illnesses.

"I spent my early childhood in Ghana, and I'm motivated by a desire to make a difference for people with major health challenges," Dr. Yvonne Greenstreet said. "Growing up in that environment, the challenges in healthcare and opportunities to improve it are so evident."

Summary

Dr. Greenstreet is one of the foremost leaders in the biotech industry with a performance sheet that not only as a woman, but a black woman, rivals and surpasses and even challenges some of the male leaders in her industry or truth be said, any other industry. Her zeal for work and pushing boundaries against all odds, is what has propelled her to the dizzying heights she occupies now, in her industry. A formidable pioneer for gender and race.

References:

Women In Biotech 2012 - www.fiercebiotech.com

Jack Bubeula

(1963)

Jack Beula was born Johnny Bubeula -Dodd to Jamaican parents, Jessiah Dodd and Johnny Bubeula, in 1963 in London, England. He attended Essendine Primary School, Quintin Kynaston Secondary School, and North London University, where he successfully completed a degree in sociology. Beula has always been interested in the history of his people and realized that if a people know their true history (both the good and bad aspects), it can help build their self-esteem, self-love, as well as pride and respect for themselves and others. Beula decided to research the contributions made in history by people of African descent and make this information available to the general public, as well as enjoyable to learn. In so doing he used the word edutainment originated by rap artist KRS-1, as an inspiration for his work.

In 1994, Beula's innovation was to create a board game he called Nubian Jak. Nubian Jak is a type of edutainment that promotes self-pride and raises awareness of the history of African people throughout the world. Beula has also self-published the book Nubian Jak Book of World Facts. He has received a number of awards and acknowledgements for his innovative work. These include the BASE UK Community Enterprise Award, a feature in the BIS Publications' 1999 Black Scientists & Inventors Calendar, the Who's Who reference book, and Caribbean Contributions to British Business publication. In 1996, Nubian Jak received recognition from Time Life Magazine and the National Association for the

Advancement of Colored People (NAACP), for its contribution to arts and culture.

Since the first European edition of the Nubian Jak board game in the 1990s, Beula has gone on to create the World Edition in 1996, Millennium Edition in 2000, and the International Anniversary Edition in 2006. In commemoration of the 60th anniversary of the Empire Windrush's arrival in Britain from the Caribbean, a special Windrush Edition of the game was launched.

Jack Beula is working hard promoting his brand; he has created the Nubian Jak Plaque Scheme, honouring pioneering black people who have made an impact on British life and culture.

Summary

Jack Beula's invention demonstrates that you can create away to make the learning of African history not only interesting, but also fun to the point of not even realising that you are learning about people, places, events and inventions. It's our hope that young people will be inspired by his creation and build upon it so as provide 21st century products which teaches African history that young people use.

References:

Black Scientists & Inventors Book 2, M. Williams & A. Henry, BIS Publications, 2003, 05, 07.

Chi Onwurah

(1965)

Chi Onwurah was born in 1965, in Newcastle upon Tyne. Her English mother was born in Wallsend, Newcastle and her father in Nigeria. Her parents met when her father immigrated to the UK; he worked as a dentist while studying at Newcastle Medical School. Her parents married in 1950, and after Onwurah was born, the family moved to Awka, Nigeria, when she was still a baby. But soon after, the Biafran Civil War started, so the family left Nigeria for England, leaving her father, who was in the Biafran army, behind.

As a child, her mother would take her to the science museum where she was inspired by the great engineering creations. She was particularly motivated by a ship called the Turibinia. She thought it was beautiful and a magnificent feat of engineering. The Turibinia was created in 1894 in Newcastle and was easily the fastest ship at that time; in fact, it was aptly nicknamed The Ocean Greyhound. It demonstrated how that era's new technology, second generation steam ships, could employ turbines to power ships.

Onwurah was part of the only black family living on a predominantly white working class council estate. She not only stood out because of her colour, but because, as she remembers, "there were no scientists or engineers living on the estate so my fascination with the science, engineering and math appeared very strange to those living on the estate, but my friends would have to take me for what I am." It was at the tender age of seven that Onwurah first knew that she wanted to earn her living from science and engineering as it was these subjects that inspired her. She completed her formal education at the local comprehensive attaining A-levels in math, physics, and further math.

Onwurah was interested in politics and it was at 16 years old that she first seriously got involved by joining the Labour Party. She was also active in the Anti-Apartheid Movement and spent many years on its National Executive.

Onwurah left Newcastle to read electrical engineering at London University's Imperial College. At that time she felt quite intimidated, as she was far away from home and most of her peers were public school educated white males. That did not deter her from completing her studies as she completed a BEng (Hons) in electrical engineering and an MBA in business administration. Some of her professional qualifications are Chartered Engineer and Fellowship of Institute of Engineering and Technology.

One of Onwurah's proudest moments was during work at a telecommunications company where she worked for 20 years. It was a product she designed and developed, using a printed circuit board (PCB), which allowed over 32 telephone calls to be made simultaneously. At the time, this was cutting-edge technology and was the foundation for others to build upon; the amount of simultaneous calls that can be made on today's equivalent area size PCB is about 1500 calls.

Onwurah believes that there are not nearly enough black scientists and engineers. She thinks the reason for this is because the ones that are around are not visible enough; also in schools there are not enough black math and science teachers. It's all of these things that help inspire young black children, she says.

Onwurah is currently the shadow cabinet minister responsible for social enterprise, digital government, and cyber security. Prior to joining the office she had the post of shadow minister for science innovation and digital infrastructure. She is also Newcastle's first black MP.

Summary

Chi Onwurah, MP believes that regardless how well or bad a child does at school, it's never too late to get into science or engineering. She says, "You can start at the very beginning, that's one plus one equals two. If you can understand that, you can go forward step by step to learn the skills you need to have a role in science and engineering."

She also shows that science is not only for men but women can and do play a major role in the sciences.

References:
en.wikipedia.org/wiki/Chi_Onwurah
chionwurahmp.com/about-me/
open.ac.uk/openlearn/science-maths-technology
Financial Governance for Innovation and Social Inclusion, 2013

Dr. Samantha Tross

(1968)

"Reach for the stars...You just have to have self-belief. Expect knock backs. It will be part of the course. If you expect them, then when they inevitably occur, you are not stressed or disappointed."
- Samantha Tross.

Samantha Tross was born to Sammy and Gwendolin Tross in 1968 in Georgetown, Guyana. Her father was a government accountant, and her mother a lecturer in health science. Tross is the second child of four; her parents gave all their children both an English and an African name. Tross' African name is Zoisa, which means "sweet child."

Tross enjoyed her early childhood in Guyana; she would often have fun reading, playing, and running outdoors with her friends. Her parents held education in high esteem and believed that their daughter should receive a good disciplined education; therefore, Tross was sent to a very good primary school run by nuns. Her parents were her first role models and so she followed their belief of a good education and applied herself in school. At the age of eleven, Tross left Guyana with her parents to live in the UK. This transition was a difficult time. As well as being in a foreign country, she was also sent to a boarding school, which meant she would be away from her parents. Tross recalls "It taught me to be self-sufficient." She was a good student at school, mostly because she worked hard and made sure she got through her courses.

In addition to doing well academically, she also excelled in sports. She was a talented athlete and competed for her school in track and field. One of Tross' greatest moments at school was winning the Victrix Ludorum at the Independent Schools Championships in 1982 and becoming a national champion in the long jump in the same year. Tross' sports teacher felt that she should specialize in the heptathlon event, as she would be good enough to make it to the Olympics one day.

Tross finished school in 1987 with A-levels in biology, chemistry and applied math. At this stage she was finding it difficult to balance both her sporting and academic ambitions. She had to make a life-changing choice; her parents wanted her to pursue an academic route and from a very young age she wanted to become a doctor. She also enjoyed partying with her friends, which would leave little time for athletic training. With this in mind, she chose the academic route. Tross went on to study at University College London Medical School. There she had many challenges during her journey. One of her challenges was focusing on her studies. As she was burning the midnight oil, her friends were out partying and socializing. Other challenges included studying in a very male-dominated environment and others discouraging her from training to be an orthopaedic surgeon.

These reasons did not deter Tross, however; with faith and support from her family and a focused mind, she pursued and finally persevered. Tross graduated in 1992 with a Bachelor of Medicine/ Bachelor of Surgery (MBBS) degree, qualified as a surgeon in 1997, and completed her higher surgical training soon after. Tross is the first female British Consultant Orthopaedic Surgeon of African Ancestry and is also a Fellow of the Royal College of Surgeons.

Tross specializes in Adult Reconstructive Surgery, otherwise known as Hip and Knee Replacement. In 2008, Tross won the Clinical

Excellence Award for service to the hospital and National Health Service (NHS), which is above what is expected in her current role. She continues to improve herself as a doctor and strives to achieve a better balance between work and life.

Samantha Tross shares her knowledge and skills by being a mentor to many African Caribbean students. She also examines the finals at Imperial Medical School, Imperial University and travels to African countries such as Nigeria, where she is involved in teaching basic surgical skills.

Summary

Dr. Samantha Tross' story is an interesting one that both children and parents can learn from. At school some people- mostly parents or teachers may push you into either sports or academics. Therefore forcing you to make a choice very early in your life of either academia or sports. Tross shows us that you can excel at both and instead of choosing one or the other early in your life, you can chose both and develop all round as a person. Enjoying what God has given you while young because there's plenty of time to make that final grown up decision.

References:

Black Scientists & Inventors Book 2, M. Williams.
Simply The Best, M. Williams and AAD

Dr. Margaret Ebuoluwa Aderin-Pocock

(1968)

Despite not fitting the common image of a 'serious white male scientist', she made it - and her message to others is simple: "Believe in yourself, and you can achieve so much."

Dr. Margaret Ebuoluwa Aderin-Pocock, fondly known as Dr. Maggie Aderin-Pocock, was born in North London in 1968 to Nigerian parents. Her mother and father emigrated to the UK for better job opportunities and to continue their studies. Aderin-Pocock 's father studied science and was keen on medicine. Aderin-Pocock, being one of four girls, always felt that her father wanted a son that would aspire to be some sort of scientist. She decided at a young age that, although she could not be a boy, she would try to make her father proud by being the best in science that she could be.

Aderin-Pocock's mother and father separated when she was just two years old. Both Aderin-Pocock and her sisters lived between their parents. She was sent to boarding school, but changed schools 13 times within 14 years because money was always tight. This constant movement, along with her dyslexia, affected her education. All this resulted in Aderin-Pocock being held back a year and often put in lower sets at school. She most likely would have left school with no qualifications had she not believed in her own abilities in science.

Aderin-Pocock also remembers telling a teacher that she wanted to be an astronaut, but the teacher felt that science would be too difficult for her and suggested she try nursing instead. However, she did not allow that teacher to determine her future; her love of science caused her to practice science at home with her father, and she soon became very good at it.

She recalls that when she moved from her old school to a new one, the new teachers did not know about her past and so were unaware of the low science set that she had been in. She used that opportunity (along with confidence built from scientific practice with her father) to convince the new school that she was good at science and should be placed in a higher set. Her cause was further helped when she was able to answer a difficult science and math question that all the other students could not.

Aderin-Pocock had a childhood desire to study the universe, and in particular the moon, so whilst many children were out playing football or skipping in their spare time, Aderin-Pocock was reading, learning, and teaching herself how to build a telescope. This she achieved at the age of just fourteen.

Aderin-Pocock finally left school with four A-levels in chemistry, physics, biology, and math. She then attended Imperial College London where she completed a BSc in physics in 1990 and a PhD in mechanical engineering in 1994.

Since graduating, Dr. Aderin-Pocock has had a very exciting career. She has worked both in the private and public sectors. She has been both a consultant and a host for science programs on television and has also acted in the famous British sci-fi TV series "Doctor Who". In 2009, Dr. Margaret Aderin-Pocock was awarded an MBE for her services to science and education.

Summary

Dr. Aderin-Pocock's life so far has demonstrated that regardless of what others think, you have the ability to attain what you want if you truly believe in yourself. Aderin-Pocock showed that even being held back a year at school and being dyslexic are not excuses to not achieve all that you could academically. With belief in herself, an interest in science, and hard work, Aderin-Pocock has reached the top of her field in science and has been recognised as such with her recent receipt of an MBE. Believe you can and you can.

References:

http://en.m.wikipedia.org/wiki/Aderin-Pocock _Aderin-Pocock

BBC Radio 4 interview.

Dr. Charlotte Armah

(1968/70)

Charlotte Armah was born in Northwest London after her parents emigrated from Ghana in the 1950s to seek better opportunities. Armah, her siblings, and parents all first lived in a house with very little space until they moved to a slightly larger one. Armah attended the local school in Turnham Green, and then in 1982 attended Ellen Wilkenson comprehensive school.

Both her parents, in particular her father, kept drumming into their children the importance of education. Her parents felt at the time that if they had had the opportunity to attend school in the UK when they were young, they would have done much better. With that in mind, they did not want their children, in particular Charlotte --being the first born in the UK--, to miss that opportunity that was not afforded to them.

As a child, Armah enjoyed science and math, but unlike many children at that time who loved the sciences, Armah did not do much extra curriculum science work out of school. You would not find her dissecting a spider or performing some form of experiment with Coca-Cola and caustic soda at home on a Saturday; she would rather sit in her room reading science-fiction, listening to music, following the pop charts, or going out with her friends.

From 1988 to 1991, Armah attended Sussex's University to study a BSc (Hons) in medicinal chemistry and then attended the University of Southampton to take an MSc (Hons) in biochemical pharmacology from 1994 to 1995. Finally, she attended the Institute of Food Research - University of East Anglia in 1996 and completed her PhD in food biophysics in 2000.

During her professional career, Armah worked in chemistry, then moved to pharmacology, and at present is in nutrition. Although she finds, at times, that she may be the only person of African origin where she works, she has not allowed that to knock her confidence and says that "Most of the people that I'm working with are educated, intelligent, and friendly."

Armah works very closely with the general public at the Institute of Food Research as she helps run experiments involving human volunteers to learn how foods, especially broccoli, can protect people from diseases such as cancer and cardiovascular disease.

Armah says, "Working as a scientist as I am, is a brilliant job. It's varied - one day is never the same as another. I get to travel. I get to meet all sorts of people.... Science energizes and enthuses me, but I also like to entertain and be social."

Summary

Dr. Charlotte Armah shows us that you don't need to go to Eton and come from a privileged background in order to achieve much in later life. You can be from a council estate and still achieve great things if you so desire and work for it. Also having supportive parents can also be an added bonus. It was Armah's father who kept drumming into her the importance of education and made sure she took advantage of the free schooling afforded to her in the UK.

References:
https://royalsociety.org/policy/projects/leading-way-diversity/inspiring-scientists/charlotte-armah/ http://news.ifr.ac.uk/2014/05/inspiring-scientists-nls/ https://www.linkedin.com/pub/charlotte-n-armah-phd/19/49a/b70 https://m.youtube.com/watch?v=4sE8qeKJIPA

Dr. Charlotte Armah

"Working as a scientist as I am, is a brilliant job. It's varied - one day is never the same as another. I get to travel. I get to meet all sorts of people.... Science energizes and enthuses me, but I also like to entertain and be social."

- Dr. Charlotte Armah

Dr. Uchenna Okoye

(1969)

Dr. Uchenna Okoye is probably London's only black female cosmetic dentist. She has three dental spa practices in Harley Street, Gloucester Road and, Goodge Street. Her high end practices offer her patients massages and manicures in the chair, shiatsu, and skin revitalisation. Okoye says, "When someone has their teeth done, my team and I get involved with make-up, hair, clothes, that whole shebang." In recent years Okoye has become nationally recognised due to her appearances as the resident cosmetic dentist on Channel 4's makeover show, '10 Years Younger' and being featured on the TV advert for Oral B Pro Expert Premium Gum Protection.

Uchenna Okoye is of Nigerian parentage and was born in Nigeria in 1969. When she was six, she moved with her family to London, England.

After qualifying from Guys Dental School in 1993, she worked at Boots Chemist when it first branched into dentistry, then joined a team at St. George's Hospital treating difficult restorative cases referred by other dentists. She is one of an elite group with a master's degree in aesthetic dentistry as well as a membership in the American Academy of Cosmetic Dentistry.

An incident during her childhood involving a dentist sparked her scientific journey. She is quoted as saying, "I was six. The dentist came up to me with something I thought was an ice cream cone.

Instead he pulled a tooth out without an anaesthetic." The result is that she never forces a client to go further than they want to. "I'll never show impatience because I know what it's like to have to deal with such a deep-rooted fear."

On the subject of ever having encountered racism, she is quoted as saying, "There have been a few moments. But it comes down to that family ethos of be the best. People will always want the best, no matter what colour or what sex you are."

Okoye opened her first London Smiling practice off Goodge Street ten years ago with the help of her family and her husband.

She believes it's smiling that transforms us. It boosts your immune system, lowers blood pressure, and releases endorphins (natural pain killers) and serotonin. People with fabulous smiles are perceived as more attractive, intelligent, and wealthy, and her company is called London Smiling.

Dr. Uchenna Okoye has twice been voted European Professional Black Woman of the Year.

Summary

With Dr. Okoye, we encounter a different motivator, that of an incident during her formative years that, in others, could have led to lifelong traumatic effects. But Okoye made it part of her purpose and used it to propel her to the high status in her chosen career that she now enjoys with a promise to never mistreat or cause her patients discomfort. She is one of the best and not just in the UK.

References:

www.standard.co.uk/lifestyle
www.londonsmiling.com

Dr. Mark Richards

(1970)

"I love to experiment with sound waves (DJ & remixing) in much the same way as I enjoy research into the behaviour of light waves (spectroscopy). Both can stimulate the mind and provide a deeper insight into our physical world but from very different perspectives."

Dr. Mark Richards was born in 1970 in Nottingham to Jamaican parentage. Richards was raised in a single-parent home by his mother. His mother knew the value of a good solid education and so encouraged Richards to do well at school. He remembers her saying to him, "Education is your passport out of poverty."

Richards, by his own admission, says he was lazy at school until a significant turning point that would shape his future career. Richard recalls, "I did a chemistry test at school and ended up getting the top marks in the class; it was a surprise to me, a surprise to the teachers and also a surprise to the top students. But what was really surprising was the 'boffins' - the ones who usually get top marks were disgusted and one even asked the teacher to check to see if he had marked my particular work correctly." At that point, Richards said to himself "why not?" Why can't someone like me get top marks? This became a driving force throughout his career. He achieved high grades at school and went on to study chemistry at Manchester University where he gained a BSc degree.

He later studied at Imperial College London where he gained a

PhD in physics. His thesis focused on the spectroscopic study of nitric acid vapour for atmospheric remote sensing retrievals.

After completing his PhD, Richards worked in finance. He returned to Imperial in 2002 as a post-doctoral researcher within the High Energy Physics Group to manage a technology transfer program. He is now a senior lecturer (fellow) at Imperial College London.

For many years, Richards has been involved in African Caribbean issues. For example, whilst at university, he founded the university's African Caribbean Society. He has worked with Tony Sewell's Generating Genius, Michael Williams' Black Scientists & Inventors program, and he is also a part of an elite UK-based network of African and African Caribbean engineers and scientists. Richards is also an active member of Imperial as one the university's Race Equality Advisory Group and also sits on their Equality and Diversity Committee. He has travelled to both the Caribbean and Africa delivering presentations on aspects of science.

Richards is a keen mix DJ who has worked on West London's community radio station Unique FM. He is also known by the name DJ Kemist, the name he gave himself after discovering that the word 'chemistry' comes from the word Kemet, which was the original name for Egypt and means 'land of the black people'. He has also set up Xtremix, which is his own independent record label.

In 2008, Richards co-founded the company Duvas Technologies, which works in partnership with Imperial College as one of its commercial concerns. Duvas is a company that specializes in wire air sensing networks for real-time pollution mapping. During Richards' time with Duvas, he has made some of the world's first discoveries and inventions. He has developed leading-edge solutions to monitoring gases and pollutants in the air, an area of research called spectroscopy.

Summary

Even though it may have been difficult for Mark Richards' mother raising her children on her own, she managed to instil good discipline and learning habits in her son. She was also a good role model for her son, having shown him that hard work, belief, and discipline pay off. Mark Richards also shows us by being a mix DJ and scientist, that a child can choose both the arts and science as they both can co-exist.

References:

Naming And Role Model - highlighting African British Role Models 1907-2007, Kwaku, published by BTWSC. http://www.imperial.ac.uk/AP/faces/pages/read/Home.jsp?person=Richards .richards&_adf.ctrl-state=glf4wnwjy_3&_afrRedirect=1990004754526000&_afrLoop=1990886196021000&_afrWindowMode=0&Adf-Window-Id=w0

Jon Chase

(1980)

Jon Chase was born in London, England in 1980. Both his mother and father were from the Caribbean island Barbados and immigrated to the UK in the 1960s. His mother worked as a nurse within the NHS, and his father was a mechanic. Chase grew up with his two older brothers in Wembley, London.

As a child, Chase was keen on chemistry sets and electronics kits and enjoyed solving puzzles, especially logic problems. He was also inspired by children's television programmes on science. Having an inquisitive mind, he would always try to seek the truth in religion and science. He remembers, after watching one of those science programmes, asking his mother, "How come scientists say that man has his genesis in Africa over millions of years ago, but at church the minister says in the Bible man's genesis is not in Africa and man is only 6000 years old?" He never got a convincing answer and so chose science to try to explain it.

He attended Twyford CofE High School in Acton. At school, Chase did not find academic studies particularly difficult, but he does remember having difficulties in planning, time management, and focusing. "I didn't find school to be too much of a challenge. Academically I was okay, but I lacked focus and never really felt like I developed an adequate study method. I was good at working things out so could usually catch up with anything I missed or hadn't studied effectively for. I also tended to get absorbed into doing one thing rather than planning out my time and activities evenly to get different things done. As a result I would often not get things completed on time or if it was on time it wouldn't be of a quality that I was more than able to achieve."

At school, Chase's favourite subjects were science, math, English, drama and religious education. In math, he excelled to a point that the teachers did not know what to do with him except give him number cards, as the textbooks were too easy for him. When he changed schools, it seemed as if the teachers had low expectations for him as they automatically placed him in low math groups; he had to start at the beginning of a math book even though he had a talent for the subject. This could have easily arrested Chase's development in math and science, but he did not allow it. Instead, the young Chase just worked even harder in those subjects until they realized halfway through the year that the books were too easy, at which point they skipped him forward a book.

He again experienced low teacher expectations of him when he went to high school. He was automatically put in a lower group for math than his true ability. Again, through hard work, Chase was sent to the top group, a group he believes he should have always been in. Today he is quite philosophical about his academic experience. He says, "I don't know if it was the result of bad communication between the schools, or misguided expectations on their part but it seemed to be a trend that I don't think should have occurred. "

Chase left school in 1996 with six GCSEs and then went to college where he took A-levels in physics, pure math, and computer science. But his poor planning skills, time management, and focus had a negative effect on his coursework, resulting in low A-levels grades. Fortunately, he got into Kingston University in 1998 where he earned a BEng in aerospace engineering. He completed this course in 2002. Chase was not happy with the class of degree he obtained and so decided in 2004 to take a second undergraduate degree in science and science fiction at the University of

Glamorgan where he achieved an upper second class honours in 2007. He then went on to earn a master's in communicating science at the same university and finished in 2008 with distinctions.

After graduating, Chase worked at the university as an associate lecturer from 2009 to 2010. He then became self-employed where he uses his many talents to communicate his knowledge of the STEM subjects to young people. In his unconventional teaching methods, he is able to excite young people into the science, engineering, and math. He runs what he calls street science and also teaches science using hip hop culture. This is interesting as this culture is made up of five basic elements: rap music, scratch DJing, break dancing, graffiti art, and knowledge/wisdom. He uses two of them to make STEM exciting for young people (rap music and knowledge).

Chase has performed his science raps at the Science Museum, the Royal Society, the Royal Institution, and at many theaters, libraries, and science festivals UK-wide. He has been on many children's science programmes, including BBC's Bite Size performing his science raps and demonstrating his street science. The Guardian identified him in 2008 as education's "Next Best Thing" after producing a science rap video for NASA about astrobiology.

Chase admits that he has had challenges along his way in science, but he will not allow anyone to hold him back, and he does not make excuses for his own shortcomings.

Summary

Jonathan Chase's message to young people is: "Education aims to pass knowledge from one generation to the next but it isn't there to provide us with the answers, it's there to help us learn how to provide the answers for ourselves. Science is just a tool for improving the quality of our answers."

References:
Interview with Jonathan Chase.

Jon Chase

Dr. Eyman Osman

(1981)

"...Genetics was at the time a very new and exciting field within the scientific arena. I wanted to know more and it was very exciting..."

Dr. Eyman Osman was born in the African country of Sudan on 2nd February 1981. Her parents named her Eyman, which in Arabic means faith. She emigrated to Newcastle in the UK with her parents Nourh and Professor Mohamed and four younger siblings in 1992. Unfortunately, the family experienced some racial prejudice whilst in Newcastle, so her father, nudged by Eyman, decided to move the family to London.

She remembers feeling "... London is where I want to be and London is where we stayed." When Eyman arrived in the UK she could not speak a word of English, but she soon picked up the language.

Osman attended Quintin Kynaston School, Marlborough Hill. Whilst at school, her favorite subjects were drama, science, and music. She particularly excelled in the sciences, helped mostly by her mother and father. As she recalls, "My parents had a very large influence over my academic career. My father completed his master's and PhD here in the UK and he is now a professor in agriculture in Sudan. Education was always an important part of our family dynamic. My mother was also a teacher in Sudan and also offered much support and help with my earlier studies."

Osman left school with 10 GCSE's, which included English language at (A) grade, not bad for someone who could not speak a word of English a few years prior. She also gained A-levels in chemistry, biology, and psychology. In 1999, she attended Queen Mary's University of London where she studied for a BSc in molecular biology; three years later in 2002 she passed with a 2.1 grade.

During the years between 2002 and 2007, Osman made herself busy gaining practical experience in her craft through paid employment and volunteering. She says, "My working career was always a work in progress for me and I made my way through the 'maze' by taking on volunteer work or internship opportunities that I came across during my summer school holidays... I have also been influenced by my friends and faith (Islam). When I thought the load was too heavy it gave me the power to believe in myself when I needed to pick myself up and carry on."

Osman returned to academic education in 2007 where she attended the Royal Free Hospital & University College London Medical School. There she studied for a doctorate in liver-directed gene transfer of atheroprotective human Apo lipoprotein AI and variants. She completed her course successfully with a thesis in the novel field of gene therapy and received her PhD in 2009.

To date, Osman has had a number of papers published in scientific journals, including an article published in a chapter of a book, and is a pioneer in mutation and gene therapy research. Osman is also an entrepreneur; she successfully established and runs a consultancy company, Faith Consultancy, with aims of sharpening and clarifying the areas of research in science through integrating arts and culture with traditional sciences.

When asked if there is a glass ceiling in science or being a black entrepreneur in science, Dr. Eyman Osman replies, ***"If there is, I ignore it and keep moving onwards and upwards. I currently own and run my own consultancy company in Science Research and Education."***

"...Genetics was at the time a very new and exciting field within the scientific arena. I wanted to know more and it was very exciting... "

Dr. Eyman Osman

Summary

Dr. Eyman Osman's message to black British children in particular and all children around the world in general is to surround themselves with people who will inspire, support, and help them develop their interests, careers, and passions. She advises them to pick one of these people as a mentor at each stage of their life and career:, as a teenager, university student, and adult.

References:
Interview with Eyman Osman.

Yewande Akinola

(1985)

Just mention the Titanic project, which involved the rebuilding of the infamous ocean liner on UK TV, and you will find that Yewande Akinola has captured and made a huge impact at a very young age -- not just fifteen minutes of fame but a whole series.

Akinola was born to Nigerian parents in Nigeria, West Africa in 1985. She first intended to pursue a career in architecture, but after a lengthy career discussion with her mother, she took an engineering path instead. Academically, she may have excelled in any field.

Akinola was accepted and enrolled into arguably one of the best colleges for engineering in the UK, Warwick University, where she studied Engineering Design and Appropriate Technology, attaining her first degree in 2007. In 2009, she took an MSCAT in Innovation and Sustainability at Cranfield University specialising in environmental engineering, and finished in 2011. She was then employed by one of the largest and internationally renowned engineering firms, ARUP. By this time Akinola had already cut her engineering teeth at Thames Water.

Akinola has been involved in varied projects, playing a key role in the development of sustainable products and water supply systems on projects in and outside the U.K. Professionally, her interests lie in the development and use of applied technology whereby she delivers improvements and solutions to projects she has patented. Examples of these include a passive rainwater collection system and rainwater outlet development that is at the leading edge in the industry. Both her patents were registered in 2005.

Apart from her engineering works, Akinola also dabbles in media work, extolling her industry. Other works she has been involved include

- Hot and cold water systems
- Above and below ground drainage within buildings
- Research into energy and renewable technologies and their patterns of consumption
- Energy consumption reduction per year (ways that help improve the system's performance thus helping save on operational costs for the buildings)

Honours:

2009 Young Engineer of the Year

2012 UK Young Woman Engineer of the Year (IET)

2012 Exceptional Achiever Award AFBE-UK, ACE

Summary

Yewande Akinola is a young woman who has blazed a trail of such high calibre and is recognised internationally, her work having led her to countries in Africa and further. Her focus and design was due to having lived in her native Nigeria and seen the need for better energy use and conservation as consumption soars globally. She is a fine example of an unassuming role model and is seen and heard encouraging young girls to choose careers in science. Solutions from the young

References:

www.arup.com
www.talent2030.org

Tony Waithe

(Unknown)

Tony Waithe was born in Kendal, Cumbria in England before moving to London. His parents emigrated from the Caribbean to set up their own business as entrepreneurs running hairdressing shops.

As a young boy, Waithe joined the Air Cadets. He remembers that during school term breaks, the cadets would have to help man the RAF museum in Hendon, London. During his time there he became inspired in math and engineering by what he saw. He was excited to see the various aircraft, particularly the Harriers; it reminded him of the aircraft on the TV programme Thunder Birds. He loved the way it took off on a vertical trajectory.

Waithe studied engineering, science, and business studies at North London College.

Waithe is a serial inventor. One of his inventions is a type of bicycle saddle he calls the Sylinder Saddle. It is named that simply due to its cylindrical shape. During Waithe's research on current standard bicycle saddles, he found that many restrict blood in the pelvic area and can cause impotence in men and produce pain and loss of sensitivity in women. The Sylinder Saddle also can be used to store spare inner tubes, tools, and a first aid kit. In 1999, his Sylinder Saddle won him a bronze medal in an inventors' competition in Geneva.

The invention that he is most known for is a type of fire escape ladder. He was inspired to develop this invention after the house he grew up in, which was situated on a high level within the Chalkhill Estate, caught on fire. Fortunately, the family was able to put it out. But it did make him wonder 'What if?' He realized at that moment if they could not put the fire out and access to the door was blocked, they all probably would not have made it out alive. This spurred him to invent his fire escape ladder. Like most inventions, after the initial idea, it was very difficult making the invention both practical and functional. The problem was that for the ladder to be of practical use, it had to be light and flexible, but this made it unstable and the rungs of the ladder lay too close to the wall. Each time he developed the ladder he noticed a flaw in the design; this was until he had a dream in which he saw the solution. He jumped out of his sleep at 4 a.m. and jotted down what he saw in his vision on paper. The solution he saw was to design the ladder as a flip over, so that when not in use it would sit clamped below the escape window and could quickly be flipped over and out the window safely in one movement if needed.

Waithe's fire escape ladder won him much fame. He was invited on all types of television programmes, including Matthew Kelly's (Eureka) Dreams Do Come True. But to his surprise, even with his newly found fame, he found that as a young black man from a council estate it was not easy to be taken seriously by financial institutions and companies. It was an uphill challenge to win investment for his inventions. He struggled for over two years trying to win it with many setbacks. He believes that he experienced prejudice along the way, but Waithe thinks that intelligence always defeats ignorance. Waithe persevered, and eventually he won funding to build a proto-type of his invention, which led to his first real sale to Kensal Rise Library in London. His fire escape ladder has gone on to be praised by the DTI, a previous British Prime Minister, and the British Safety Council.

Waithe runs a young inventors' club in which members of the

club go into schools to help inspire young people to explore math, science, and engineering. He believes that black children may not be motivated to go into STEM areas simply because of a lack of confidence. He thinks that if they were exposed to more black people in these areas, such as on TV or in schoolbooks, it would have a positive effect on their minds and boast their confidence to study STEM.

Summary

Tony Waithe's advice to wannabe inventors is, "if you get a great idea then why not enter an inventors' competition?" He has personal experience of this as he has entered several, which includes the prestigious British Inventors Show where he won a gold medal for his invention. Although, as a black inventor, Waithe has experienced many challenges, his attitude is that he will never give up., He says *"You have to champion your cause."*

References:

open.edu/openlearn/body-mind/the-z-files-benjamin-zephaniah
Waithe, making valuable Inventions in the 21st Century
ITV1's The Big Breakfast
Carlton TV's Your Shout.

"...When a man has done what he considers to be his duty to his people and his country, he can rest in peace. I believe I have made that effort and that is, therefore, why I sleep for the eternity..."

- Nelson R. Mandela.

Dr. Chris Imafidon & The Brainy Bunch

(A family that practices STEM together, stay together)

Dr. Chris Imafidon and Ann Imafidon came from Edo State, Nigeria, to London over 30 years ago. He is currently working as a renowned scholar and international education consultant to several governments. He also serves as a mentor and coach to American students at various academic levels using Skype and web technology.

Unlike all the other scientists mentioned in this book, Dr. Imafidon offers a different perspective in that as much he has a portfolio of achievements that is extensive and leaves one wondering what more can such a man achieve, we find that his genius extends to his family, mainly his children.

Part of Dr. Imafidon's expertise is in the field of education, and in this field he is renowned the world over with papers and publication galore. His methodology is revolutionary and has been proven time after time in that he has helped transform educational/learning patterns in individuals, groups, and institutions.

Quote: **"If you really want a child to learn anything, find out the best way that child learns," says Imafidon in a story on Black America Web. "Every human being has a unique way of learning."**

The children are the proof of the pudding in this instance by virtue of their remarkable achievements in their own right, mentoring from parents to the older children, who in turn mentor their younger siblings. Chris and Ann Imafidon have five children: Anne-Marie (25), Christina (20), Samantha (16), and twins Peter and Paula (13).

Anne-Marie:
the eldest child, is multi-lingual. She speaks six languages and graduated from college at age ten. At 13, she was the youngest person to pass the U.K.'s A-level computing exam. She went on to attend John Hopkins University in Baltimore and got her master's degree from Oxford University, all before she turned 20 years old. Just last year she was called a "serial world record breaker" in the September 2011 edition of Higher Education Digest. Anne-Marie has mentioned that she believes in mentoring children to help them succeed. She is involved in the STEM (Science, Technology, Engineering, and Math) program to help fulfill the need for math and science female leaders. She is currently working in a high-level position at an international investment bank in the United Kingdom.

Christina Imafidon:
was the youngest student in history to attend a British university – the United Kingdom University. Christina is now working as an intern with the Citigroup Corporation as well as conducting research on mathematics with Oxford University.

Samantha Imafidon:
passed two high school-level mathematics and statistics exams at age six. She became the youngest girl in the UK to attend secondary school at the age of nine. Samantha was the sibling who mentored the twins to pass their own math secondary school test when they were also six years old. She is a gold level champion in the 100m and 200m relays.

Peter and Paula:
are the UK's current highest achievers. At nine years old, they made history as the youngest children in British history to attend high school. They are now in their third year. The children became the youngest to ever pass the University of Cambridge's advanced mathematics exam after participating in the Excellence in Education program. They set world records when they passed the A/AS-level math papers. Peter Imafidon, who is also a 100m and 400m relay champion in London, has said that he would like to serve as Prime Minister one day; and his sister Paula, a county champion in rugby, would like to teach math. Both students are also keen musicians.

Summary
A family that works together succeeds in their endeavours. The parents practice what they preach and take a very keen interest in their children's education and well-being. In this family we find the ultimate secret to success. As much as we praise and applaud individual success, it's only in witnessing such familial progressive living that gives the rest of us hope for the future of humankind and our youth. This family should be a template for the wider communities, and their successes should be duplicated as they transverse all manner of boundaries.

References:
Imafidon - demipost - Apr 2013
Black America web

AUTOSAFE
HEIGHT

"I would like to inspire children to believe in and try to achieve their dreams." -

- Peter Sesay.

Time Line 3 - Modern History

Time Line 3
Modern History

- **1939 - Ron Headley** is born in Jamaica
- **1939 - Dr. James S.R. Russell** dies
- **1940 - Geoff (Godfrey) Palmer** is born in Jamaica
- **1944 - Prof Sir Bernard Ribeiro** is born in Ghana.
- **1947 - Dr. Harold Moody** dies
- **1948 - Dr. Arthur Wint** becomes an Olympic gold medalist, winning the 400 meters at 1948 Summer Olympics.
- **1948 - The Empire Windrush** sails from Jamaica and docks at Tilbury on 22nd June, with 492 Caribbean people, invited to the UK to help rebuild the country after WW2.
- **1950 - Pauline Straker-Rodgers** is born in Jamaica.
- **1950 - Jerry Yamoa** is born in Ghana.
- **1950s - Dr. Tim Tavares** is born in Jamaica.
- **1953 - Dr. James Jackson** Brown dies.
- **1958 - Nottingham racial disturbances**
- **1958 - Notting Hill Riots (London)**
- **1959 - Antiguan, Kelso Cochrane**, is murdered by a gang of white racists in Notting Hill, shortly after midnight on 17th May 1959, whilst walking home. His killers are still at large.
- **1959 - Leeroy Brown** is born in London.
- **1959 - In response to the Notting Hill riots activist Claudia Jones** organizes a Caribbean festival at St Pancras Town Hall London. It was a precursor to the Notting Hill Carnival.
- **1960 - Dr. Elizabeth Rasekoala** is born in Nigeria.

- **1960 - Dr. Donald Palmer** is born in London
- **1961 - Peter Sesay** is born in London.
- **1962 - Jamaica** receives independence from Britain, many other Caribbean countries under British rule soon follow.
- **1963 - The Bristol Bus Boycott,** led by Paul Stephenson and the British West Indian Council.
- **1963 - Dr. Yvonne Greenstreet** is born in Ghana
- **1963 - Jack Bubeula** is born in London
- **1965 - The Race Relations Act of 1965**
- **1965 - Dr. Chi Onwurah** is born in Newcastle.
- **1966 - Dr. Allan Powell** Goffe dies
- **1968 - The Race Relations Act** of 1965 is strengthened
- **1968 - Dr. Samantha Tross** is born in Guyana.
- **1968 - Dr. Margaret Aderin-Pocock** is born in London.
- **1968/70 - Dr Charlotte Armah** is born
- **1969 - Dr. Uchenna Okoye** is born in Nigeria
- **1970 - Dr. Mark Richards** is born in Nottingham
- **1976 - The second Notting Hill Riots**
- **1976 - The Race Relations Act of 1976**
- **1980 - Jonathan Chase** is born in London.
- **1980s - Dr. Tim Tavares** invents and innovates a type of High Temperature Super Conductor Technology. The same decade his invention is a feature in London's Science Museum.
- **1981 - The Toxteth Riots (Liverpool)**
- **1981 - Dr. Eyman Osman** is born in the Sudan

- **1981 - The Brixton Riots** (April 11th) Sparked off by the shooting of Cherry Groce.
- **1981 - The New Cross Fire,** 13 black children who attended a birthday party at a house in in New Cross, London are burned alive in an arson attack on the house. Many believe that it was racially motivated. Till this day their killer(s) are still at large.
- **1982 - Dyke & Dryden create the annual "Afro Hair & Beauty Show"**, the marketing and educational wing of the company.
- **1983-84 - Sam King** who sailed on Empire Windrush from Jamaica to England in 1948, becomes 1st black Mayor of Southwark, London.
- **1985 - The Toxteh Riots (1st October)**
- **1985 - The Tottenham "Broadwater Farm Riots", (6th October)** sparked off by the death of Cynthia Jarrett, after police raid her house.
- **1985 - The Brixton Riots, (28th to 29th September).**
- **1985 - Yewande Akinola** born in Nigeria.
- **1987 - David Simon** creates the Ebony Education Supplementary Schools
- **1990 - Nelson Mandela** - Freedom Fighter, is freed from captivity by the South African Apartheid government on 11th February.
- **1991 - Dr. Elizabeth Rasekoala** received a commendation from the Commonwealth Association of Science, Technology and Mathematics Educators.
- **1991- Roland Adams** is murdered by a gang of white racists, in south east London which is racially motivated (similar to Kelso Cochrane murder three decades earlier - 1959).
- **1992 - Professor Charles Ssali** invents Mariandina, which is a treatment for HIV/ AIDS
- **1992 - Dr. Sir Arthur Wint** dies in Linstead, Jamaica.

- **1993 - Steven Lawrence** was a black teenager from Eltham, south east London, murdered by a gang of white racists, while waiting for a bus on the evening of 22 April 1993 (similar to Kelso Cochrane murder three decades earlier-1959) most of his killers are still at large.

- **1993 - Prime Minister & Freedom Fighter Nelson Mandela of South Africa,** visits Neville and Doreen Lawrence. From that moment on, the London Metropolitan Police begin to take the murder of their son Stephen seriously.

- **1994 - On 26th April all South Africans finally get the chance to vote in a free and fair election.**

- **1994 - Jack Bubeula**, creates the game Nubian Jak.

- **1995 - Ron Headley** invents the Eco-Charger.

- **1995 – The Million Man March** in Washington D.C. On 16th October.

- **1997 - The best-selling Black Scientists & Inventors series of books is launched - Book 1, being the first of the titles.**

- **1998 - Ron Headley** is offered £6 Million for the 'Eco-Charger' from a major French automotive company.

- **1998 - Jerry Yamoa** creator of Yamoa Powder ™ (taken from his Grandmother) is featured in the Press and on National TV News.

- **1998 – The 10,000 Man March,** in London's Trafalgar Square on 14th October.

- **1999 - Tony Waithe** wins the World Bronze medal from the 'Salon Inventions' in Geneva. It is the largest International Inventions Exhibition.

- **2000 - Leeroy Brown** files for a patent for his combination Air Pump - Car Jack invention.

- **2002 - Leeroy Brown** wins the "Consumer Award" on the BBC TV show Tomorrows World for his combination Air Pump-Car Jack invention.

- **2004 - Professor Charles Ssali** dies in Uganda.
- **2005 - Anthony Walker** is racially murdered in Liverpool by Michael Burton and cousin Paul Taylor.
- **2005 Peter Sesay** wins £100,000 investment from Dragon's Den Investors, for his patented invention, the Seat-Belt Height Adjuster.
- **2006 - Christopher Alaneme** is stabbed to death in a racist killing in Kent.
- **2007 - British then Prime Minister Tony Blair issues a Statement of Regret** for the trafficking and enslavement of African People in the Caribbean & Americas for over 200 years by the British. An official apology and redress has still not been made since 1834 till now (2014)
- **2007 - On 7th February, Levi Roots** wins £50,000 investment for his creation Reggae Reggae Sauce from the Dragon's Den Investors.
- **2008 - Jerry Yamoa** dies
- **2008 - Professor Bernard Ribeiro** is Knighted for his outstanding work in science.
- **2008 - Dr. Samantha Tross**, Orthopaedic Surgeon wins the "Clinical Excellence Award" for Services to her hospital and the NHS.
- **2008 - Pauline Straker-Rodgers** wins the "Dollcrafter Excellence Award".
- **2008 - Dr. Mark Richards**, co-found the company Duvas Technologies, a company which works in partnership with Imperial College as one of its commercial concerns.
- **2009 - Peter Sesay** dies in London.
- **2009 - Dr. Margaret Aderin-Pococks** is awarded an MBE for her services to science and education.
- **2009 - Michael Williams, author of the best-selling Black Scientists & Inventor books,** delivers a historic presentation on the subject at London's Science Museum on 29th October.

- **2010 - Chi Onwurah** is elected as the Member of Parliament for Newcastle upon Tyne Central. She is Newcastle's first black MP.
- **2011 - Mark Duggan** shot dead by the police on 4th August, in Tottenham, London. The second Tottenham Riots sparked off by the death of Mark Duggan. The riot spreads throughout England and some other parts UK. It was first called the Tottenham riots, then London riots then finally the UK riots. (August 6th onto August 11th).
- **2012 - Yewande Akinola** Awarded young engineer of the year UK.
- **2013 - BIS Publication** host a presentation in Tottenham on the Contribution of Black Scientists & Inventors in the UK, over one and half years before this publication.
- **2013 - Chi Onwurah** becomes Shadow Minister in the Cabinet Office (Labour Party).
- **2013 - Making Freedom Exhibition Launched by Windrush Foundation** (August 1st) in London UK (Marcus Garvey Library in Haringey)
- **2014 - Dr. Geoffrey** Palmer is Knighted for his outstanding work in science.
- **2014 - Arthur Torrington CBE and the Windrush Foundation's Making freedom Exhibition,** Marking 175 years of emancipation in the British Caribbean is installed in the Houses of Parliaments during June that year.
- **2014 - Black Scientists & Inventor in the UK** book by Michael Williams and Manyonyi Amalemba is published - (the first of its kind to be researched and written in the UK).

KEEP
BRITAIN
WHITE

Part VI: Chapter 7 -

The African / Caribbean Inventive & Innovative Musical Influence on Britain

CHAPTER 7

The African / Caribbean Inventive & Innovative Musical Influence on Britain

In music, the African contribution to the UK is both rich and historically embedded. It's a contribution that can still be heard, felt, and seen to this present day. Most likely, music of some sort (be it humming using the human voice or tapping stones together) has been around for as long as man has inhabited this planet.

We look to Africa simply because it is the birth place of modern man and again we find African civilizations inventing musical instruments. It goes without saying that when most people think of Africa and music, the first instrument that comes to mind is the drum as it plays a very important role within African tradition. They have been used as oracles, griots, broadcasting stations, defence systems for war cries, and for metaphysical purposes as well as for entertainment. As can be seen, the drum and music in general, was not compartmentalized in

African societies but instead was treated holistically. It was and is still a major part of life from birth to death within the African community. Due to the modern compartmentalization, we now only see it in terms of art. But in as much as it is art, the ideas to create, design, and produce musical instruments requires an understanding of the sciences, mathematics, and engineering -- an understanding of the properties of sound, sound waves, frequencies, and timing.

According to C.R. Gibbs in his book 'Black Inventors', there is evidence that Africans during pre-historic times in North Africa enjoyed music, using both string and drum instruments. The San people in the south of Africa would use the string on bow-and-arrow weapons to make music; they later invented an instrument called the gwashi, which is a stringed instrument with either 5 or 4 strings (ramke) for male and female players, respectively. The gwashi is similar to a hand-held harp and considered a predecessor to the modern guitar. Images can be seen featured on South Africa postage stamps of rare musical instruments issued in 2011.

In east central Africa, they invented instruments such as the marimba, which is made of wooden slats of differing lengths placed over a hole in the ground or a hollow log/gourd [sound-box]. It's beaten by harder sticks to produce sound; some say the modern-day piano is based on the marimba. The original marimba is similar to the West African xylophones.

The Africans are also credited with inventing the banjar, which they brought to America as enslaved people; it eventually became the banjo. In other parts of Africa, instruments such as an early type of flute and the Kaffir piano, also known as the kalimba or mbira, or gourd, hand piano were invented in Zambia/ Zimbabwe/South Africa.

Musical instruments and musical style inventions would notably appear in the UK when Africans first migrated from Africa to that region. Apparently, the Moors brought a form of music and dancing to the UK. Some historians believe that it was the Moors who introduced Morris dancing; others such as Mac Ritchie believe the original African inhabitants of the UK introduced it. Other commentators say that the bagpipes originally came from Spain and were brought to Scotland by the Moors.

Amongst the black poor of London during the 1820s there were many black musicians who went on the streets as entertainers in order to make money to live. Among these were the Ethiopian Serenaders. At this point we borrow from text that was kindly submitted to us via Kwaku, of the Black Music Congress. If we look at what the Moors brought to Briton, we find the 'oud', a parent of the lute and maybe even a forerunner to the modern guitar.

Earlier in this book we spoke of trumpeter John Blanke, himself a Moor, who played in the courts of both Henry VII and Henry VIII. Another Moor, a contemporary of Blanke, played in the Scottish court of James IV. He was a drummer; although there is no name on records, they do show a moryen taubranor (old Celt term for black drummer) having received payment from King James IV's account. There is also mention of a choreographer - a Moor as well (Source: National Archives).

Ignatius Sancho lived between 1729 and 1780 and is mostly known for his work as an abolitionist during the British abolition of slavery movement. A lesser-known fact is his work as a musician and published composer in the UK.

George Bridgetower lived between 1778 and 1860 and was born to a German mother and an African-Caribbean father (possibly Barbadian) in Poland. As a child he successfully conducted violin concerts in Europe and Britain. The British Prince Regent (later George IV) took an interest in him and oversaw and paid for his continuing musical education. Between 1789 and 1799 he played over 50 concerts in London theatres, which included those in Convent Gardens, Drury Lane, and the Hay Market. An admirer of his was one Ludwig Beethoven, who dedicated his composition "Kreutzer Sonata Violin No.9 in A Major" to him.

In England, Bridgetower married Mary Leech Leeke in 1816 and continued his musical career, teaching and performing. He was elected to the Royal Society of Musicians on 4 October 1807, and attended Trinity Hall, Cambridge, where he earned the degree of Bachelor of Music in June 1811. George Bridgetower had a successful career in music and conducting in the UK. He died in 1860 in Peckham and is buried in Kensal Green cemetery.

In the late1800s and early 1900s Britain was alight with

the talent of Samuel Coleridge-Taylor, born in London to a father from Sierra Leone or Nigeria (a brilliant physician) and an English mother. Coleridge-Taylor studied the violin and composition at the Royal College of Music in London. He won awards and prizes everywhere in the UK, and leading composers of that time noticed him. He performed at venues such as the Royal Albert Hall, and at the end of his performances he was recalled many times by the audiences who would not leave without the all-important encore. Samuel Coleridge-Taylor is famous for his composition "Hiawatha's Wedding Feast, Songs of Slavery, African Suite" circa 1898. When he died he was referred to as the "greatest musical sensation", and others compared him to Beethoven.

According to Kwaku, in 1872 the Jubilee Singers (also known as the Fisk Jubilee Singers) travelled to the UK from America to fundraise through performances for a new university called Fisk, which was to become one of America's historically black colleges. Whilst performing in England, their audience included ordinary fans, but also Queen Victoria. Their songs included old Negro spirituals such as "Steal Away" and "Swing Low, Sweet Chariot", which ironically has become the English national rugby team's anthem.

In the 1900s ragtime and jazz were introduced to Britain from African-American bands such as the Southern Syncopated Orchestra, when they performed in England and across Europe. The orchestra was later replenished with both Africans from the continent and the Caribbean. Some of these artists later went on to spread jazz across Britain.

Samuel Coleridge -Taylor

It should be noted that many artists from the British Empire would come to London to record and have their records pressed, and from London the records would be shipped back to their respective countries and around the empire for sale. Kwaku says, "For example, Kumasi Trio came to London in 1928 to record for the British record company Zonophone, a version of 'Yaa Amponsah' now a High life classic, which was then sold in Ghana."

There were countless more African musicians and composers between the 1700s and the 1900s in the UK that we could mention, but they are out of the scope of this publication. Suffice it to say that their contributions can still be felt today.

The African-American musical contribution is huge and has shaped UK's current popular culture to present day and looks like it will continue to do so for generations to come. It should also be noted that the music from African-Americans was not only brought to the UK by them, but also by people from the Caribbean that had been listening to and imitating the music of North America for years. They also created their own brand of this popular music. For example, two styles of African-American music are blues and rhythm & blues, which many music historians believe came out of, or at least was highly influenced by, the black church's gospel music. This wass similar in the Caribbean -- the style and expression of the music was influenced by the gospel music of their churches. This may be one of the reasons that African-American music was so attractive to Africans in the Caribbean. In Jamaica many of the recording artists had cover versions of African-American records in their own style of mento, ska, rock steady, and reggae.

With travel to the UK from America and the Caribbean during the 1800s (as slave trade was coming to an end) and in particular the 1900s (especially after the emancipation both in the Americas and the Caribbean), England would gain a plethora of African diaspora music styles. If we look at post-Windrush (circa 1948), it can be argued that it was Africans that introduced rock and roll to England. Many English people thought they knew what rock and roll was when they heard the likes of Bill Haley, Pat Boone, and Elvis Presley, until the likes of Chuck Berry, Fats Domino, and Little Richard were unleashed on them.

It was at this point doing the 1950s and 60s that many British acts (that went on to be internationally famous making billions of pounds over their combined musical careers) were studying and copying African-America / Caribbean music inventions, innovations, and styles. You only have to listen to some of the biggest artists to ever come out of the UK on what they have to say about their influences: Tommy Steele, Cliff Richard, the Beatles, the Rolling Stones, the Animals, Tom Jones, Englebert Humperdinck, Dusty Springfield, Rod Stewart, Eric Clapton, Lulu, etc. just to name a few. So you should be able to see from this paragraph that if Elvis Presley is known today as the king, then African musicians of that time were the king makers.

African-American guitarist Jimi Hendrix, who lived in England during the 60s and 70s and died in London, can be said to have been one of the main drivers of UK popular music. He changed the way an electric guitar would be played forever as none of the aforementioned musicians can deny his influences on their musical careers. Others like Muddy Waters, BB King, Chubby Checker, and Otis Redding, who spent some time touring the UK and with UK musicians, also had major influences on British artists. We cannot talk of African-American influences without mentioning women such as Etta James, Aretha Franklin, Tina Turner, and the whole Motown experience. Often forgotten is a singer, songwriter, and virtuoso guitar player who predates and has been noted as having had a strong influence on all the preceding greats -- a lady by the name of Sister Rosetta Tharpe, also known to be the first to successfully cross over from gospel to popular music with a number of hit records. This grandmother of rock and roll was born Rosetta Nubin in Arkansas, USA in 1915 and died in Philadelphia in 1973. At her height of fame, she toured Europe and UK in 1964 with Muddy Waters.

The undisputed godfather of soul James Brown's band introduced a drumming pattern. Brown's style of funk was based on funky bass lines, drum patterns, and syncopated guitar riffs. His musical innovations had a huge impact on the rhythm section of many British bands. He is also been advanced as an innovator of hip-hop that has permeated the younger sectors of British society.

Other influences were from partially home grown talent, in that the musicians had settled here after playing their part in World War II in various capacities but found little joy on returning to their home colonies afterwards. Some eventually found their way back through UK colonial office recruitment efforts after the war to help rebuild the British economy (Windrush plus generation). However, entertainment was key for mind and soul for the new arrivals and pay was quite good in this industry. So many musicians switched day jobs for night jobs. They had a profound impact as they travelled across the land to earn a living and entertain. Musicians such as Emily Ford & the Checkmates, Cuddly Duddley, the Southlanders, and Winifred Atwell (also a trained pharmacist), were popular in late 50s and through the 60s, all whose members mostly came from all over the Caribbean islands and settled in the UK. You also found Calypsonians such as Lord Kitchener and jazz musicians Dizzy Reece who both came over on the Windrush. There were jazz musicians such as Joe Harriot, Shake Keane, Harold McNair, and the Trinidadian Edmundo Ros, who came with a Latin style, all adding a new flavour to British music for future generations – both black and white.

Would the Beatles have been one of the greatest rock / pop bands ever with out the help of Harold Adolphus Phillips (Lord Woodbine)? We really don't know! We know that Harold was their earliest influence, but it should be appreciated that Paul and John developed a unique style and talent. The Trinidadian singer-songwriter was also the Silver Beatles (as they were known then) first manager, mentor and influence. He gave them their first break in a nightclub he managed in Liverpool and was first to show them how to perform black music.

An instrument was developed and designed by Africans in Trinidad and Tobago and widely considered as the only new musical instrument to be invented in the 20th century; it is widely used today in all manner of music due to its versatility and adaptability. It has also been incorporated in modern synthesizers and other keyboard technologies, and its sound can be heard both in pop and rap music. It is the only instrument that follows Pythagoras' calculated formula for all musical instruments (cycles of fourths and fifths). The instrument we are referring to is the steel pan (idiophone) -- a percussion instrument but not a drum (membranophone). It is and has been the backbone of most carnival celebrations worldwide, including our very own Notting Hill Carnival in London, the largest carnival in Europe. This instrument transferred a whole culture to the UK as it introduced not just the music, work for costume designers, steel pan makers and players, the dance, the tunes and the food, but also almost always carries a little of the Caribbean with it wherever it is played.

The ska music from Jamaica would introduce a new form of music to the UK with the likes of Millie Small's international hit record "My Boy Lollipop", Toots and the Maytals' "Pressure Drop", and Prince Buster's "Madness" of the 1960s. Later in the 1980s this musical sound would resurface and influence new generations of English bands such as the Specials, the Beat, and Madness who incidentally had a hit with Prince Buster's "Madness" and "One Step Beyond".

The influence that reggae music has had on music throughout the world in general and the UK music in particular should not be understated. One only has to look at artists such as Bob Marley, Peter Tosh, and Jimmy Cliff, plus far too many others to mention in this piece. The UK Punk Rockers movement also pays tribute to the influence of reggae music. This was demonstrated in the Clash's punk rock cover version of Junior Murvin's "Police & Thieves".

In the 1980s and 90s, the children of the Windrush generation would invent a new form of reggae music, which was dubbed lovers rock, influenced by the reggae music of their parents, the rhythm & blues music of the US, and their own UK experiences. These new British-born lovers rock artists went on to influence white UK artists. You can very much hear this influence in the music of UK artists such as the Police, Culture Club, Amy Winehouse, Adele, etc.

Bass culture is very much rooted in African music and travelled to the UK though reggae music in the Caribbean and hip hop music from America. It's our belief that popular dance music such as UK hip-hop, acid, acid house, jungle, hard core, UK garage, dubstep, bassline, and grime all have an African root. The backbone to most African music as we stated earlier is the drum. The drum produces low frequencies that cannot necessarily be heard more than they are felt. It's a kind of spiritual thing -- frequencies that speak to the human spirit. At a presentation some years ago at the science museum, former Steel Pulse band member and music lecturer Mykaell Riley is reported to have said that the bass of the drum resonates especially with women and maybe on a sexual level even without them being aware of it. Back full circle to the beginnings of this segment

Banja

Man playing the Banjo

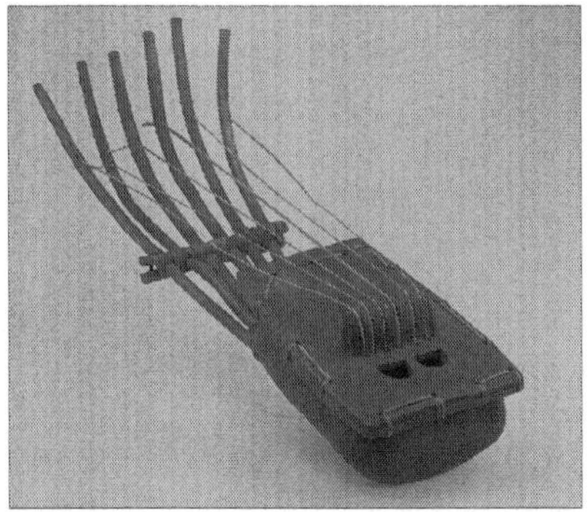

Gwashi

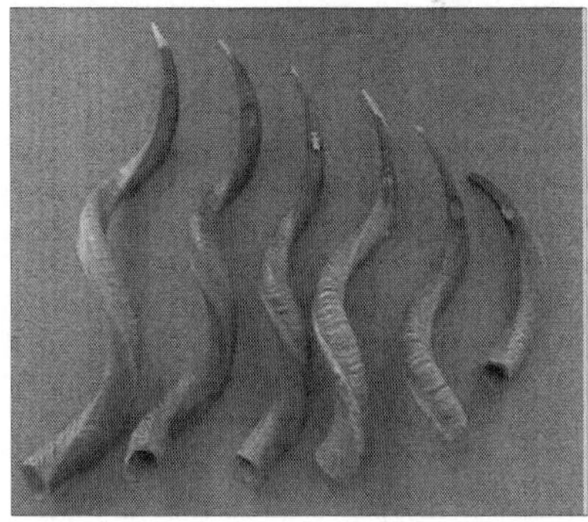

Kudu

on music and we find the heart beat that is the drum.

In order to appreciate these low frequencies and high frequency sounds, new technologies needed to be invented or at least innovated. In the 60s and 70s when Africans in the UK were having house parties, the music quality was an important part. Many self-taught African electronic and mechanical engineers built amplifiers that could produce the level of sound required: pre-amplifiers, echo-chambers, and the actuator's containers (speaker boxes) built by both skilled and unskilled cabinet makers. Until then, there was no off-the-shelf DJ equipment that could produce the sound required to give a good rhythm and blues, reggae dance session. From these parties, the early UK sound systems were developed. Out of necessity, Africans in the UK were playing with sound and sound waves, inventing and innovating equipment and music as they went along.

Multinational companies such as Sony Entertainment, Borsch, Sanyo, Blaupunkt, and others may have been studying these early sound system inventors and innovators as we started to see purpose built turntables such as Techniques SL 1200s for the art of mixing, scratching, cutting, and wheeling back along with speaker systems to handle the low frequency music produced by African musicians emerge in the latter part of the 20th century. This would also make huge impacts on in-car entertainment as again we saw in the 60s and 70s that it was young Africans in the UK that were building in-car sound systems to achieve the music quality they wanted as they drove along. This caught on to the general British young person,

A UK sound systems, 1 of 2 speaker box sections.

and years later, car manufacturing companies started incorporating good sound equipment into their new cars as standard features. This incidentally again shows the value Africans create for other people in terms of products and wealth at the expense, sometimes, of themselves.

African Drum

In Conclusion

The preceding mini-excursion into the musical influences that the African has had on the UK just goes to show in yet another small way that without the contributions of the African over the millennia to present day, the world we live in would have been bereft of the deeply spiritual, soul-touching and uplifting, and therefore harmonic influence that music brings to man and his environment. Where would we be without it?

We must not forget that with inventing and innovating different forms of music, Africans also invented the tools that created that music (including wind, percussion, and string instruments) and the sounds we all love to hear today. Much of the design and creation for the electronic system we use today to record and play music has been heavily influenced by how African youth have used or invented makeshift versions. For example, the Japanese are credited with the invention of the karaoke machine in the 1970s which in its simplest form is an instrument for producing backing music for a singer. However, in the 1950s and 60s, St. Lucian singer and amateur engineer Emile Ford invented an instrument that provided backing music, which he used when he performed around the UK.

Other examples of African / Caribbean young people in music, inventing and innovating, were those of the sound-system culture, brought from the Caribbean, Jamaica in particular, that have had a huge impact on British popular culture including night clubs, entertainers, and equipment.

References:
Wikipedia.
Black Scientists and Inventors Book 3.
Unpublished paper by Kwaku of BTWSC, 2014.
Conversations with Arthur Torrington CBE- 2014-2015.
Conversations with Byron Lye-fook, September 2014.
The Girl Can't Help It, 1950s film.
Channel 4s Deep Roots Music.
BBCs Rock n Roll Series.
Sex and Race Vol1, J. A. Rogers.

Part VII:
Chapter 8 -

Protecting Your Work

A Few Case Studies
Where Black Inventors & Entrepreneurs
Have Used Intellectual Property

CHAPTER 8

Protecting Your Work

A Few Case Studies Where Black Inventors & Entrepreneurs Have Used Intellectual Property

Historically it has been difficult for Africans to protect their creations. As already mentioned, during the transatlantic enslavement trade, Africans working on the plantations of the Americas could not own their own inventions, in fact the rights to their inventions would automatically go to their slave masters. Simply because the enslaved African was seen as the property of the slave master, so anything that belonged to the enslaved actually belonged to the slave master and this included the very dreams, visions and ideas of the enslaved African.

Post slavery 1838 in the Caribbean and 1865 in the USA, many African peoples ideas were being stolen, usurped, appropriated and even misappropriated by non- Africans. The greatest examples of this can be seen in African music of the Caribbean and Americas, such as the African creations of jazz, blues, rhythm & blues, rock n roll, samba, salsa and reggae etc. Many of the great black artistes who worked hard inventing and innovating these music styles made numerous amounts of people wealthy, but as for themselves, many died penniless and broke, leaving their families to pay the debts they owed. Some of the reasons for this were that they signed contracts without legal representation that were not in their favour or did not have a contract and generally gave up their ideas, creations and inventions all too easily, to people who knew their true value. This may be because they just did not know their true value or it could have been that during much of the 19th and 20th century, Africans in the west were just trying to survive, so whatever funds they could get for themselves and family, were welcome.

In the UK the good news is that now there are a number of Black Music organizations that have been set up to help protect the copy rights and moral rights of recording artists. In July 1985, the Black Music Association UK (B.M.A.UK) was set up by Root Jackson, Byron Lye-Fook, Gaspar Lawal, Kofi Dako, Philip Buchanan and KK Van Lare. The aim of the association was to bring together individuals and independent companies involved in the Black Music Industry under an effective umbrella and to protect and promote the interests of all those involved in creating, producing, promoting and distributing Black Music within the music industry(Byron Lye-Fook, 2014).

Kwaku set up a similar organizations called The Black Music Congress They work to deliver training and intergenerational community events. Its website covers black music, with a bias towards British artists and products, music industry education, and music industry issues. (BBM website, Kwaku 2007)

In the next few pages we discuss Intellectual property such as copyright, trademarks, franchising and branding (Trade dress). We use case studies (their life stories) of prominent African/Caribbean business persons in the UK to illustrate this point.

Intellectual Property (IP) 101

Your thoughts can be a valuable asset if used correctly. They are a property of your intellect and most wise people protect their property from theft. Below we give some basic information about intellectual property and the laws governing it. What is Intellectual Property (IP)? It can be described as a product of your intellect or mind.

There are four main forms of IP, they are: Patents, Trademarks, Designs and Copyright.

Patent

This is derived from the Latin "Letter Patent". It protects an idea and its implementation. It is concerned on what the thing is, what it does and how the thing works.

Trademark

A trademark™ or service mark ® is a Word, Symbol, Brand Image or Goodwill, it is anything that is non-functional used to distinguish products or services of one company from another. It ties the goodwill and reputation of the company to its own product and or service. A trademark gives you strong monopoly rights and can last indefinitely. It prevents others trading off association of your product or service. In some countries before you can use the trademark it must be registered with a government agency.

Designs

Designs refers to the appearance and non-functional aspects of a product, design patents protect the design for 3 years automatically within the European Union and 10 years in the UK – from first marketing.

Copyright ©

In the UK copyright law states that once your idea (story) is out of your head and on paper, computer, e-mail etc. it is automatically copyrighted. This law protects work such as manuscripts for books, lyrics for music, scripts for television & radio and computer programs. The law states that your work is under your ownership until death plus 70 years. This law may differ in countries outside the UK and the law does change so you may have to get an update.

"Please note that the above is just a basic guide. If you have invented anything, written a book, play, created a system or company name etc. that needs protecting, then it is advisable that you get a book on IP Law or seek an IP specialist or lawyer."

A Word On Those Inventing Whilst Working For Companies

When working for a company and in particular companies involved in Research & Development, most employees are asked to sign various contracts before they are accepted for the position, such as Non-Disclosure Agreements and others which state that anything the employee creates, discovers and invents, belongs to the company and so the company owns the RIGHTS.

References:
Self Publish Successfully- A 20 Step Guide, Michael Williams, 2014, BIS Publications.
Protecting Your Number One Asset, Michael Lechter.
http://www.45-rpm.org.uk/dire/emilef.htm
Wikipedia
Black Inventors
Unpublished paper by Kwaku of BTWSC, 2014
britishblackmusic.com website.
Conversations with Byron Lye-fook, September 2014.

A Few Case Studies Where Black Inventors & Entrepreneurs Have Used Intellectual Property.

Terry Jervis

Terry Jervis (1962) - Film and Television, Copyright and Branding

Terry Jervis was born in 1962 in Hackney, East London to a Jamaican mother and a Guyanese father, both of whom immigrated to the UK in the 1950s. He grew up with his two brothers and two sisters; sadly, his youngest sister died young. Jervis attended Upton Park School in 1973.

As a child Jervis wanted to become an astronaut, although his mother wanted him to become a teacher. Jervis spent part of his leisure time drawing and being fascinated with early television sets that had been recently introduced to the UK. He recalls fondly, "...my older brother Paul brought home one day some cine-film and we put it in this cartridge thing and rolled it and we could see the moving images.".

When his parents separated, Jervis, along with his brothers and sisters, was brought up by his mother, who was a typical West Indian woman -- a disciplinarian. As a boy from a working class background, Jervis knew the importance of reading. It was something that his mother instilled in him. When you are growing up with only one bread winner, your mother, there is not enough income for you to do all that you would like to do such as travelling, going to the cinema, or shopping. Jervis found enjoyment in books; with books he was able to travel anywhere he wanted, even to space. Jervis says, "It was books that helped me develop my imagination."

From the 1960s to the early 1990s, seldom could black faces be seen on British television. Whenever one was on, in an advert or film, the whole African-Caribbean family household would run to the TV to see the character before he or she was killed off. Jervis remembers one such incident when he observed the effect a black character had on his family; this led him to say to his mother, "One day I'm going to make films."

At the tender age of 14 years, Jervis travelled to the US to purchase Marvel comics, which he religiously collected. But on this occasion his intention was to buy in bulk at a low price and take them back to the UK to sell to public school boys at a profit; he knew their parents had the money. This cash he would reinvest in a film he was making for his mother. The film was called "The Sam Cooke Story" about a musician his mother loved. Jervis thought it was a great way to make money with education and creativity. Jervis rose to control a department at the BBC, and at the time was one of the youngest and one of a handful of black people. There he would direct, produce, and even present a range of programs. During the 1980's he produced the Yoof TV programmes "Behind the Beat" and "Def II"; and in the early 90s he produced the extremely popular comedy series "The Real McCoy," which, incidentally, took its name from African-Canadian inventor Elijah McCoy (see Black Scientists & Inventors Book 1 by Michael Williams for more information). In 2002, he produced a documentary about tennis aces Venus and Serena Williams entitled "Raising Tennis Aces: The Williams Story."

Jervis also directed a musical programme, which featured stars such as Michael Jackson and Stevie Wonder. He also ran his own record label Down To Jam and invented both a cartoon and game "Spirit of the Pharaoh" based on a concept he had on a flight back from the Caribbean sitting next to and talking to Sir Richard Branson. When the concept was finally created, Branson had massive point-of-sale images of the Black Pharaoh in his flagship business Virgin Mega Stores.

Jervis also produced the incredibly popular children's musical theatre production "Tropical Island." If you look at any of Jervis's ventures, in particular "Spirit of the Pharaoh" and "Tropical Island", you can't help but notice that he takes particular care to its branding and produces many spin-offs based on the one concept; additionally, he makes sure all his creations are trademarked.

Jervis, a keen Marvel comic collector and fan, oversees the branding rights for the UK of some of Marvel's famous superheroes such as Spider-Man, The Incredible Hulk, Iron Man, and the X-Men. He also worked with the Royal Air Force after he convinced them that he should take care of their branding and merchandising.

What Can We Learn From Terry Jervis' Story?:
He's a creative and entrepreneurial spirit; also Jervis did not allow his background to stop him from dreaming, visualizing, and taking actions that would have a huge impact on himself, his family, and millions of people throughout the UK and world. Please note the importance Jervis placed on reading and how it helped develop his own imagination.

References:
Interview with Terry Jervis, 2011.

Levi Roots

Trademark and Product Branding

Keith Graham is a reggae musician, chef, and entrepreneur who was born in Clarendon, Jamaica in 1958 as the youngest of six siblings. Keith Graham later changed his name to Levi Roots because as he states, "I'm not Scottish, but my name is; it's down to the slave masters that were in Jamaica at the time. That's part of the reason I changed my name and because, when I was young I used to look in the mirror and think, you don't look bloody Scottish."

After his parents immigrated to the UK in 1963, Roots was brought up by his grandmother until 1969, when he joined his parents in Brixton, London. When Roots arrived in the

UK he could not read or write. He also remembers, "When I was young I never had money. My parents couldn't afford Christmas or birthday presents; they couldn't even afford to send me to school." He goes on to say "...so I enjoy the fruits of my labour now..."

Roots had a 25-year career as a successful reggae artist and performed with great artists such as James Brown and Maxi Priest; he was also a close friend of Bob Marley. Roots performed "Happy Birthday, Mr. President" to Nelson Mandela in 1992 in Brixton and was also nominated for a MOBO award in 1998.

In his spare time, Levi Roots made and sold his family sauce that he called Reggae Reggae Sauce (jerk barbecue sauce), which was particularly popular at the famous Notting Hill Carnival.

In 2007 Roots appeared on the BBC television programme "Dragons' Den" seeking financial backing for his Reggae Reggae Sauce using his grandmother's secret recipe. At this point it should be noted that Roots was taken to court in 2011 by his ex-business partner, who claimed that Roots stole his sauce invention and passed it off as having come from his grandmother. According to the verdict of the case, the sauce wasn't invented by his grandmother; in fact, he made up the story as it was a good marketing ploy, but it was actually invented by Roots himself.

On the "Dragon's Den" programme, Roots delivered his pitch in the form of a reggae song, and he won over £50,000 of investment from angel investors Peter Jones and Richard Farleigh for a 40% stake in his company. Soon after the programme, Sainsbury announced that they would be stocking his Reggae Reggae Sauce in 600 of their stores.

His business is currently worth £30m and growing, and his brand can be seen on other sauces he has developed, on pizzas, ready meals, and drinks. You will also find his brand on food sold in fast food chains such as KFC and Subway.

Levi Roots opened a Caribbean restaurant called Rastarant, and his first cookbook was published in 2008.

As of 2014, Levi Roots' latest venture is to launch a multimillion-pound chain of restaurants throughout the UK and Jamaica. Levi Roots lives in South London with his family.

ReGGae ReGGae sauCe Jerk/BBq

What Can We Learn from Levi Roots' Story?

Again we can see that Levi Roots is using the influences of his brand (Reggae Reggae Sauce) to place value on other products to create new worth. It should also be noted that if you create a joint invention, then you put both a gentleman's agreement and a written agreement in place to avoid any disagreements in the future.

References:
Black Entrepreneurs In The UK, (Williams & Soso: 2008),
Wikipedia.
The Sunday Times, Money, Fame & Fortune, Donna Ferguson. 2014.

Dyke and Dryden

Product Branding and Event Branding

Dyke and Dryden is a story about three young men who travelled from the Caribbean, where they were born, to the UK in order to economically better themselves and their families. In 1965 Len Dyke and Dudley Dryden, both from Jamaica, set up the company Dyke and Dryden in North London, UK. The business initially sold and distributed records; however, hair and cosmetic products for women of colour were later introduced on the product line. In 1968, Anthony Wade from Montserrat joined Dyke and Dryden. Anthony Wade acquired a third share of ownership in the company and was given the role of marketing director. After intense diligence on the company's finances, the directors decided to focus their attentions on retailing, distributing, and manufacturing the hair care and cosmetic side of the business.

Dyke and Dryden later opened several retail, wholesale, and cash & carry outlets in London and Birmingham. They were pioneers in the UK and Europe black hair care industry, setting up the first retailing, distributing, and manufacturing outlets. They helped generate hundreds of thousands of jobs in the black community as well as other communities in the UK, including chemists, distributors, sales agents, retailers, hairdressers, delivery drivers, accountants, computer programmers, graphic designers, event management teams, and more. Dyke and Dryden became the largest black-owned business in Britain during the last three decades of the twentieth century.

In 1982, one of their young talented employees Rudi Page was sent on their behalf to the Bronner Brothers trade show in Atlanta, GA and came back with a great idea based on what he had seen. They set up a subsidiary company called Afro Hair & Beauty Ltd., a name coined by Page. This company has hosted the very popular annual Afro Hair & Beauty Show at the Grosvenor Hotel, Alexandra Palace, and the Islington Business Centre. Wade says that "... Afro Hair & Beauty is an organization dedicated to the education, development and promotion of ethnic hair care in

Britain, and it remains the shop window of the industry."

Dyke and Dryden focused on providing good customer service, innovating existing products, and creating new ones. Regardless of whether they were selling other companies' products or their own, they would make sure they carried the Dyke and Dryden brand. Wade says, "Branding is everything." In the late 90s, Dyke and Dryden sold their brand to a South African company for millions of pounds. It must be noted that Dyke and Dryden were not only about making money; they also became involved in community issues. Tony Wade, the last surviving member of the team, gives back by writing books and delivering presentations to young people on how they can also make millions.

Dryden Story

What Can We Learn from Dyke and Dryden's Story?

Dyke and Dryden took branding and trade marking to another level. They created a separate company to concentrate on marketing and growing their brand, Afro Hair & Beauty Ltd. They were also able to teach the general public about their products, while maintaining market leadership and increasing their revenue. They knew the value of the brand that they were creating as they were able to sell both companies for millions.

References:

Black Entrepreneurs In The UK,(Williams & Soso, BIS Publications, 2006.
Interview With Tony Wade, 2006.
How The Made A Million, T. Wade, Hansib Publications.

David Simon

Franchising and Trademark

David Simon was born in 1958 in London to parents who emigrated from the Caribbean Island of Carriacou to Kilburn in London, England in 1956. In England, his father worked as a postman and his mother looked after home and family. Simon, along with his other siblings, attended Kingsgate Primary School where they all excelled academically. In 1967 the Simon family moved to South London, so Simon had to start a new school. He performed poorly and remembers not learning much there, so he left school with few qualifications. Simon was eager to make up for his lack of qualifications so he attended the local further education (F.E.) college, and within a short time he gained enough A levels to take his desired course at the University of Greenwich in 1979, where he read humanities and completed in 1983 attaining a BA Honours Degree.

Whilst at university, Simon was introduced to all types of people, but what fascinated him most was meeting a Jamaican poet who led poetry workshops. It was the poet who introduced him to African and Caribbean literature. This had a great impact on him -- his mind was on fire and at that point he knew that he was going to be a writer. As well as his BA Honours in humanities, which he was studying at the time, he attended African studies during the evenings, where he discovered his true heritage.

After Simon completed his BA degree, he went on to complete a Master's degree in 1992. It was during this time he became increasingly aware of the educational underachievement of African-Caribbean children in UK schools; he wanted to solve this problem and so his life's work as an educator began. This led him to become a Deputy Head of an education department at a large F.E. college. He also opened a Saturday school in 1987, which he named Ebony; due to the need of such schools, in a short while he had opened several throughout London which included homework clubs. Simon says, "I started the company with the intention of just helping a few African-Caribbean children who needed extra support. We started in a rundown youth club in Catford and I remember on my very first day that there had been a Blues dance the night before in the venue that we used, so I had to clean the place with water and disinfectant to get rid of the smell of drink and cigarettes. Anyway, on that very first day we had one student, and about two years later we had about a hundred. I never thought the company would last 26 years, and I would still be working in education...Let me also say working as an educator I have realized the importance of the Science, Technology, Engineering and Mathematics (STEM) courses..."

During the mid-2000s he had a vision, one which would involve him systematizing his schools to take the daily running of each school away from him and give that to other people. He also felt that he had a great working model and a well-known brand that African-Caribbean people in the UK could invest in. Simon always wanted to create jobs for African people in the UK, so with that in mind he went about learning how he could franchise his schools.

After legal consultation he changed his trading name from Ebony Education to Simon Education, and in 2011 he started his franchise business model. Simon recalls the steps he took: "We started to franchise in 2011 to try and develop a business model that could be replicated quickly and effectively. However, though we were successful with the first few franchises we took on, we found that because they were not used to running their business, once money began to come in they simply sat back and thought that the business would run itself. So we began to experience problems with our early model of franchising. Our present model is more online-based and gives us greater quality control and reach. It is early days but things are looking exceptionally good."

Simon on the Benefits of Franchising in the UK Black Community

The benefits for the franchisee are that they are using a successful model, they have a mentor, and the whole business infrastructure is set up for them. The downside for the franchisor is that you will always get franchisees who will simply steal your resources and business and try and run it by themselves. This is very short-sighted but it keeps happening. However, the franchise model allows you to obtain investment capital and grow your business.

Simon on Branding and Trademarks

Branding and trademarks are key as they make a positive statement in the minds of your clients that your business has a certain standard and competency. Increasingly branding is about the client experience, and this is how we approach our work. It clarifies what I have to do each day.

What Can We Learn from David Simon's Story?

Simon believes that Black UK businesses have to realize that there is a massive black/African diaspora and an African continent that wants their business. We are not a minority and therefore we need to link up amongst ourselves and be brave and take our businesses to these regions. In addition, black UK businesses need to help our youth with apprenticeships, internships, and jobs. Our long-term goal has to be about building the African diaspora and laying the foundation for the next generations.

References:
Interview With David Simon, 2014.

"Successful people make more mistakes and learn from them than unsuccessful people" -

R.K.

Kanya King

Trade dress & Branding

Kanya King was born in the 1970s and was raised in Kilburn, North West London to Ghanaian and Irish parents; she is the youngest of nine children. King attended Kilburn High School.

King's father died when she was still young, and life became very difficult; there was very little money in the household, so family finance was tight. It may have been that situation that sparked the financier in her. One of her first entrepreneurial activities was the acquisition of property at the tender age of 18 years.

After completing her school education, King continued her studies at the University of London's Goldsmiths

College where she took English and drama. She went on to work at Carlton Television as a senior researcher in 1992; she was one of the founding members and part of the production team on "The Chrystal Rose Show".

King's love of black music and not seeing anything in the UK at the time that celebrated and rewarded it, made her think. After all, the contribution that black music has had on the UK both past and present was huge and should not go unnoticed. The pop music that was finding its way on the national radio and TV had its roots in black music. That said, she had a vision to see this music rewarded in the open for everyone to see.

In 1997 in a packed New Connaught Room in London exceeding the capacity of 500 to 1000 people, Kanya King founded the successful Music of Black Origin (MOBO) awards show. This award celebrates black music and music influenced and inspired by black compositions. The likes of ex-prime minister Tony Blair and wife Cherie Blair, celebrities, legendary performers, and top executives attended. The show reached 250 million people in 57 countries, and the show and the MOBO brand has continued to grow in its strength. In 1999 she joined a government committee for a music industry task force; in the same year she was honoured with an MBE. Additionally, she is a Patron of the Horniman Museum and a founding member of Net Women.

She also received an honorary doctorate degree in business from London University. Kanya King has also given speeches to young people about reducing gun crime in the UK (Williams & Soso:2008).

Permission of Kanya King

What Can We Learn from Kanya King's Story?

Kanya King is a prime example of an exceptional, strong, passionate, and utterly determined woman. She is a visionary, innovator, and an entrepreneur. She has always looked at the bigger picture, and over the years has carefully grown the MOBO brand and protected it as a parent protects their child. The MOBO has become "much more than music."

References:
Black Entrepreneurs in The UK Pack. C. Soso, M. Williams, BIS Publications, 2006.
Valiant Women, Z, Kamauei, BIS Publications, 2010.
Wikipedia

Part VIII: Chapter 9 -

How To Produce the Next Generation of Black Scientists & Inventors:

An Eleven Step Guide.

CHAPTER 9

How To Produce the Next Generation of Black Scientists & Inventors

After studying the qualities that have made the scientists and inventors (ancient and modern) and others within this book successful, we were able to ascertain eleven similar qualities that warp and weft through them all. Below we have highlighted these eleven qualities and believe that they are a good starting point to create the next generation of black scientists and inventors in the UK.

1. Create a Positive MENTAL Attitude & Create:

The theme throughout the book THINK BIG by internationally renowned neurosurgeon Dr. Ben Carson is READ. He explains how it was books and reading that helped shape the person he is today. Carson tells young people that they should read BOOKS actively and learn new words every day -- that goes for adults as well. I also want to add that it is important for all groups of people to not only read about other people's cultures and histories, but also to read about their own first, then move on to others. This is especially true for African people who have tended to read about other people's cultures, achievements, and stories before knowing about their own. I have coined this type of reading as culturally determined.

Just one more thing: I am very aware that there are some people who may not learn best from reading, but learn best from auditory or visual information, or kinaesthetically. That is also fine, as long as they are engaged in learning, growing, and seeking knowledge.

2. Think:

It was the great industrialist Henry T. Ford who once said, "Thinking is the hardest work there is. That is why so few people engage in it." If only the majority of us knew the true power of the mind when engaging the process of thinking. I have read many biographies, autobiographies, and history books on successful people including Professor Charles Ssali, the Dyke & Dryden trio, Dr. Samantha Tross, Olaudah Equiano, Dr. Harold Moody, Dr. Charles Drew, Terry Jervis, Elizabeth Rasekola, etc. All of the aforementioned, whether consciously or unconsciously, used the power of thought and POSITIVE THINKING to achieve all that they had in their careers. Tony Wade of Dyke & Dryden was invited to a presentation by the two owners before joining the company. After the presentation Tony Wade said, "Let me go away and think about it." After a few weeks of thought and visualizing where he would fit into the picture and identifying where the company was losing and making money, he decided to join. At a time when there were few black businesses in the UK, the trio used their collective positive thinking to create arguably the most successful independent black business of the 20th century within the UK. Although Sir Dr. Geoff Palmer was placed in his school's educational sub-normal (esn) unit on arrival to the UK simply because of his culture, through positive thought and attitude, he was able to transform himself out from there by hard work and determination to become an international leader in science. All the above people realized that in order to change or get what they wanted in this world, they first needed to visualize it in their head and actually believe that they would attain it, and then act upon it.

3. Believe:
Self Belief (Knowledge of Self)

Inscribed on some of the ancient African temples in (Khemet) Egypt you will find the words **'Man Know Thy Self'**. What is meant by these words? I think that the ancient Africans had an understanding of what true education was; they knew that for someone to be educated, it had to come from within and not from without. That is, to understand the outer world you first have to understand your inner world, including your own physical body and mind. Dr. Mark Richards recalls that as a child in school, he was quite lazy even though his mother kept telling him, "Education is your passport out of poverty". In one of his chemistry exams he scored top marks, which surprised him, his teacher, and his peers to such a point that the top boffins, as he called them, thought the teacher had marked his papers incorrectly and asked for the papers to be checked. But it was at this point Dr. Richards said to himself "Why not?" Why can't a person like me, from my racial group and background, achieve top marks? He goes on to say, "It's that principle that I have used to guide my career." I believe that it was at this point of achieving top marks that Dr. Richards started to develop a different perception of himself; his belief of himself started to change. He started to develop a new self; in fact, his self-belief had changed and this, in turn, changed his future forever.

4. Guard Your Mind

On a very basic level the mind can be divided into two parts; the conscious mind and the subconscious mind. The conscious mind as suggested is conscious of what it sees, hears, thinks and what it causes the body to do. Whereas the subconscious mind isn't aware of any of these yet without it our heart would stop pumping blood around the body, we would have difficulty in walking, talking, breathing and even dreaming. The subconscious mind is affected by everything that we hear, see, smell, touch and do, without us consciously knowing and It remembers everything even if we don't. It helps to form who we are, our self-beliefs, confidence and how we feel about ourselves. With that in mind be careful of what the subconscious mind takes in when listening to music, watching television or films and reading newspapers/ magazines. Make sure the music, films/documentaries and newspaper articles that go into your subconscious mind are things that are going to help enhance and build you 'a positive self-esteem and in turn a positive mental attitude.' Another note on Self Esteem - The trans-Atlantic enslavement trade, has had a negative mental effect on most people of African descent, those in the west (Diaspora), in particular and other Africans, in general.

When you study what took place during this period in terms of the mental brain washing, terrorizing and humiliation of the enslaved Africans for a period of no less than 400 years, it can easily be understood why this is. As a student and teacher of African heritage, I have found that many African/Caribbean children and their parents do not want to know anything about the trans-Atlantic enslavement trade. There seems to be, in quite a number of these cases, some sort of 'embarrassment' about what happened, as if they were the ones that enslaved, tortured and humiliated themselves. I express to them that 'you are looking at this period incorrectly' and instead of drawing strength and wisdom from this history, they choose to stay as far away from it as possible. If you are an African American or African Caribbean, then in doing this you do your ancestors a huge disservice. Why do I tell them this? Simply because when Africans were kidnapped from Africa and forced onto the ships, not everyone made it across the Atlantic. In some cases, 20% of enslaved Africans died on the ships alone, then when they made it to the plantations, the life span was between 5 and 9 years. Those that lived and were forced to procreate did not give up the desire to be free. In fact from the very beginning of the African enslavement in the Americas, Africans resisted their enslavement in the form of riots, rebellions and revolutions, until finally they forced the European powers involved in the evil trade to release them. This history of fighting for freedom and self-determination, must not be forgotten or negated as only the strongest enslaved Africans, in mind and body, survived, allowing people such as myself to be here today to tell the story. It is on their backs I stand, it is on their backs we stand. It is a strong sense of self belief that we should draw from their determination to be free. So I ask, No!, I plead with African parents - teach your children about the true history of what their ancestors went through so that we could be here today. Let us take a leaf out of Jewish tradition, when they talk about and observe their ritual 'Passover.' This reminds them every year about their Exodus out of slavery from Pharaoh, and also when they remind their young about what happened to their ancestors in Nazi Germany and other parts of Europe. Like them we can learn to forgive and let go but should never, **Never, NEVER forget, lest it happens again.**

5. Focus:

I believe that concentration and focus are twin sisters, but let me first talk of the latter. In my self-publishing courses and in my book Self Publish Successfully: A 20 Step Guide by Michael Williams, I point out just how important it is to concentrate on the job at hand and the level of concentration needed. Please let me explain: As a child, did you ever hold up a piece of paper to the sun in order to try and catch it alight by the heat of the sun's rays but found that the paper just would not catch fire? Well, even though it was a hot day and the sun was heating up a vast area, it was not being concentrated properly on that paper, so its rays were being dispersed. But once a magnifying glass was employed and held between the sun and the paper, it concentrated the sun's rays with FOCUS on that paper, and it started to burn.

6. Concentrate:

The educationalist Dr. Jawanza Kunjufu speaks about a workshop on concentration he attended while a speaker at a youth camp. The workshop facilitator had the group form a circle and placed an object in the middle. He wanted the group to see how long they could concentrate on the object without allowing distractions to enter their mind. Kunjufu says everyone acknowledged just how difficult it was to concentrate, and the workshop facilitator said the brain is like a baby -- it needs to be trained and developed (J. Kunjufu, 1986). Good concentration comes with daily practice, and it's my belief that people should be taught how to concentrate from a young age. Some of the greatest athletes, scientists, inventors, and entrepreneurs, such as Sir Dr. Arthur Wint, Dr. Samantha Tross, Dr. Donald Palmer, Peter Sesay, and Dr. Eyman Osman have learnt how to concentrate and have used it within their lives and chosen professions.

7. Failure & Fear:

Don't be afraid to fail. Understand that failure is just another side of the same coin -- the other being success. Unfortunately, as Robert Kiyosaki, the author of Rich Dad Poor Dad, says, "Our school system teaches us that failure is bad and so young people grow up not knowing the true value of failure and the true lesson that can be learnt from failure." Peter Tosh (reggae musician with the Wailers) put it this way in a song he wrote entitled "Equal Right": "... Everyone wants to go to Heaven, but nobody wants to die." George Subria, author of Getting Black Folks to Sell, makes a good point when he says,

"...most black folk lack an appreciation for how much failure most successful people experience before they find success. Most black success stories are about young people. We hear about young athletes, rappers, actors, footballers, and dancers. Many of these young people are succeeding at the first thing they attempt. But what most people don't know is that if these young people are successful in their early 20's, it's because they have been dedicated to their craft since they were children; so may have about 15 years of experience during which they would have experienced many failures. But they kept on going and became successful."

How different it would be in terms of success for young people if they took a leaf out of the examples left by some of the world's greatest scientists, inventors, leaders, and entrepreneurs such as Lewis Latimer, George Washington Carver, Leeroy Brown, Levy Roots, Colonel Sanders, Henry T. Ford, Hon. Marcus Garvey, and Thomas Edison. You may recall when Thomas Edison was asked by a journalist, "How did it feel to fail 1,000 times trying to invent a light bulb?" His reply was, "I have not failed. I've just found 1,000 ways that won't work." Overcome the FEAR of Failure by being passionate about what you are doing, as passion builds success not FEAR.

8. A Definite Purpose:

The first woman in America to become a self-made multimillionaire during the 1800s was the inventor and entrepreneur, Madam C.J. Walker. Many wonder how she did it; after all, this was just 40 years after emancipation in the US. Some critics say that she was lucky, probably just in the right place at the right time. Walker would dispute that by saying ***"...I had to make my own opportunities, I waited for no one - I got up and made my luck...!"*** Walker had a definite purpose and that was to try and halt the hair loss of women (something she had suffered herself) and to provide beauty and hair products to women of African descent, making them feel better about themselves. Haven't times changed? Hair loss then vs. hair loss now; back then, products were a remedy, but now much loss of hair is due to products (ironic!).

At the same time Walker was amassing her great wealth, the Honourable Marcus Garvey from the Caribbean island of Jamaica was also doing something special as he travelled through Central America and Europe. Everywhere he went he asked himself, "Where is the black man's government? Where are his men of great affairs, leaders, captains of industry, etc.?" Everywhere he looked he could not find them so he embarked on ***his definite purpose and decided to make them himself.*** Within a few decades, he did. Garvey created the largest African organization in the world at the time and dozens of businesses, properties, international transport facilities, international media outlets, etc. had a major impact and influence on peoples of the Caribbean, South and Central America, as well as Africa in seeking independence and gaining self-rule.

9. Confidence:

What is confidence? If we examine the English Oxford Dictionary, it defines confidence as "a firm trust; feeling of certainty, boldness." How do we get a sense of certainty? Through practice, habit, knowledge, truth, and observation. For example, if we observe the earthly cycle of night and day, after some time we can be assured that light will follow darkness. This is the same for seasons, as through observation we can be assured that the autumn will be followed by winter, spring, and then summer. The universal law of habit also can give us a sense of boldness simply because we can start doing things automatically. When a baby learns to walk, he may stumble in the early stages; however, he doesn't give up -- he keeps on practicing walking until it becomes a habit he doesn't have to think about. Students who have confidence in their knowledge through practice, habit, and the truth of a thing, normally do well on their tests and exams (and can usually remember what they have learnt 6 weeks post exams), simply because they understand, which, in turn, gives them great confidence in the subject. This also holds true for the business person, and in fact anyone for that matter, who attains those attributes in order to develop their confidence. The Honourable Marcus Garvey said about confidence:

"Without confidence you are twice defeated, but with confidence you win even before you start."

10. Steadfastness:

On dictionary.com, steadfastness is defined as "fixed in direction; steadily directed, firm in purpose, resolution, faith, attachment." I will show how steadfastness is used by the two examples below. The first example is the Great African General and military strategist Hannibal Barca of the Carthaginian Empire. It is said that during the Punic wars, when he marched thousands of his men along with hundreds of elephants from Africa to Rome via the Alps, he decided that he would literally burn his bridges after crossing them, so he and his men would be in the frame of mind of "no return, no surrender". He had only one direction and one thing in mind and that was to capture Rome.

My second example is the Africans who came from the Caribbean to Britain during the 2nd World War and others that were recruited to help rebuild the economy, health, and transport infrastructure during the Empire Windrush. Many of them experienced huge amounts of prejudice and racism in terms of housing, schooling, employment, and policing methods. When looking for somewhere to live, it was familiar for Africans to see signs in windows that said "No Blacks, No Irish, and No Dogs". But because of the determined nature of Africans from the Caribbean, they would not and could not run back to the Caribbean. Instead they fought for change by agitating, demanding, and forcing change in the UK through both peaceful and direct action methods; and because of their steadfast attitude, many of the people who now come from other parts of the world to settle in the UK benefit from their struggle for equal rights.

11. Imagination (Ideas & Dreams):

Napoleon Hill labeled this power as "infinite intelligence". He said that ideas that seemingly come out of nowhere come through "Infinite Intelligence" (Kimbro & Hill). Marcus Garvey said in his African Philosophy lessons that this was Universal Intelligence: when the human mind, which is a "unitary intelligence", is one with the Master Creator's Universal Intelligence. Haandle calls this the MIND and says that the human mind is, in essence, a small piece but exactly the same in quality as that of the MIND, which created everything from an idea or a THOUGHT.

Your thoughts are spiritual and have more power than you could ever understand. Use your thoughts positively to achieve what you will. Your thoughts can be exercised by your imagination. Exercise your imagination, ideas, dreams, and thoughts by constructive reading, meditation, or prayer.

"There is no Force like Success, and that is why the individual [Successful person] makes all efforts to surround himself throughout life with the evidence of it; as of the individual, so should it be of the nation."

The Most Honourable Marcus Mosiah Garvey.

"Young Gifted And Black--- That's where it's at" -

Nina Simone

"We can be anything we want... Passion builds success not fear.." -

M. Williams

Why we Think Black People In The UK MUST Learn How To SELL

It is my opinion that too few people understand the true value of sales and even fewer black people know the value of sales.

In the case of black people this could be a result of colonization and slavery; during these times Africans were the products being sold into slavery and resources were also being stolen from their land, during colonization, in order to enrich non-Africans. In the UK and the USA, this has been further compounded by racism in terms of lack of employment in the private sector etc. and so most employment for Africans in the west has been in the public sector where making money from face to face sales is not usual. I believe that the effects of slavery, colonization, racism and lack of job opportunities in the private sector have helped to create a sense of financial dependency of the African on the European. Today there is less belief in the mind of many Africans that they can create their own wealth now, than there was just after slavery and that also goes for African states/governments.

In the opening pages of George Subria's classic book - Getting Black Folks To Sell - he points out that "black labour is becoming obsolete in western countries, not because white folks no longer like blacks but simply because they no longer require our labour. Machines and computers can do what humans once did and also due to the global economy, black folks in the west are now also competing with European economic refugees. For examples in the UK the second and third generation of Caribbean people, whose forebears migrated to the UK in the 1940s and 50s, are not only competing with white working class, English people, but also Eastern Europeans, and those from other western European countries, in particular those from the Portugal, Italy, Greece and Spain (P.I.G.S.) regions, who travel to the UK for better job opportunities. Subria also says it's amazing how many college graduates he sees that can't get a job, so he advices that selling opens the door for blacks to create their own economic opportunities.

Let me just take a moment to demonstrate what sales can do for a community. Let's take the inventor, who invents a product, a system, service or an idea which creates value. It's then the sales person who brings that product to the market and persuades the market to part with their money in exchange for that value.

In the book industry, which I'm a part of, it is again easy to see the important role of the sales person. You see its the sales person who creates money through their sales, that funds the publisher, who can then pay the designer, printer, editor, and author and also pays the paper manufactures, the delivery/shipping company, the advertising company etc. All of this is made possible through the sales person. It's my opinion that if African people want to see real wealth then they must become sales people whether they're scientists, inventors, authors, creators of some sort, business owners or even work for other people. To get the job you desire you must know how to sell yourself, to get the grant or loan you want you must know how to sell your idea, to create a successful company you must know how to sell your services and products. Some of the richest people around are sales people, Bill Gates, Madam C.J Walker, Dyke & Dryden, Levy Roots, Steve Jobs or even Oprah Winfrey.

You see sales is the back bone to all successful ventures, black people must learn how to SELL, teach those skills in your homes, churches and supplementary schools.

"You can get it if you really want but you must try and try, you'll succeed at last." - Jimmy Cliff

What are Opportunities?

Opportunities are seen with the mind and not the eyes - this is called VISION.

Make your own opportunities by good preparation which includes education, seeking knowledge and know how, practice and learning from failure, then when the gates of opportunity open you are ready to walk through and take it.

"Where there is no vision, the people perish" - Proverbs 29:18.

Conclusion

Conclusion
Manyonyi Amalemba

Manyonyi Amalemba. In the research and development stages of this book, we discovered hundreds of black scientists and inventors that presently grace and those that have previously graced this land. Reading about their contributions to very diverse and varied scientific endeavours, work that helped the advancement of the UK and in turn the international community, certain factors became clear. These were characteristics/ prerequisite for their success in their chosen fields:

- (a) **Vision** - mostly borne out of personal experiences(often bad/negative) at an earlier point in life
- (b) **Goal setting** to follow through and achieve the vision
- (c) **No barriers insurmountable** [e.g. colour bar (racism), poverty, distance, social/economic or even study-time and application to task - lonely environment]
- (d) **Focus, Concentration and Self-belief,** runs all through their way to success
- (e) **Determination**
- (f) **Education, and the advancement** of it, held in high regard all round
- (g) **Regardless of their successes some of these eminent scientists have voluntarily given back to their communities**

Conclusion
Michael Williams

Michael Williams. It is hoped that the reader will have acknowledged the conclusive evidence that European history and African history is a shared one and that European history could not exist without Africa and the African.

It can be seen that the creativity and inventive mind of the African had not only created the first civilization and with that the first technologies, the first mathematics, chemistry and physics principals in Africa, but that the African brought that mind and duplicated those inventions both in Europe and around the entire earth.

The African has shown an enduring spirit, an unstoppable will, and a 'let's make it happen' attitude. For at least the last 500 years we have lived in a world of two minds, one is a mind from a people who have developed a false sense of supremacy (white) and the other is from a people who have developed a false sense of inferiority (black). Much of this was created by European scientists and scholars during the 15th to 19th century practising pseudo-science; concluding results based on opinions rather than scientific fact and then using propaganda vehicles to spread their opinions of Africans.

This way of thinking has created attitudes which have damaged millions of people all over the world during those 500 years. We hope that this book goes some way in addressing those attitudes, as I believe that in order to create a more just and truthful world, both the supremacy and inferiority mind-sets need to be destroyed. I hope that it is realised that we all have the ability to create both good and bad things. But if in our life time we want to create good, then we must stand on TRUTH and create from that position.

Education is not something that we receive from the outside but is something that we pull out from within.

Leaders and teachers such as the Hon. Marcus Garvey, Napoleon Hill, Henry Ford and Nelson Mandela have taught us that you don't need to be wealthy or go to a stone building to receive an education, all one needs to do is pick up a book read and then - THINK. The African will take heed of Carter G. Woodson's words and no longer will he carve out a back door to walk through, but he will walk out the front door with his head held high in the knowledge (as Jessie Jackson puts it), that "he is somebody." The 35 plus scientists and inventors found in this book demonstrate that the African can create, invent and innovate absolutely anything her/his mind conceives and believes despite all kinds of odds placed in front of her/him.

In closing, I must emphasis at this point that although both Amalemba and myself, have given our conclusions herein, this book is far from being concluded. We believe that it is up to the reader to make their own conclusions. This may even mean that the reader carries out further investigations and research to either disprove or qualify the information in this title.

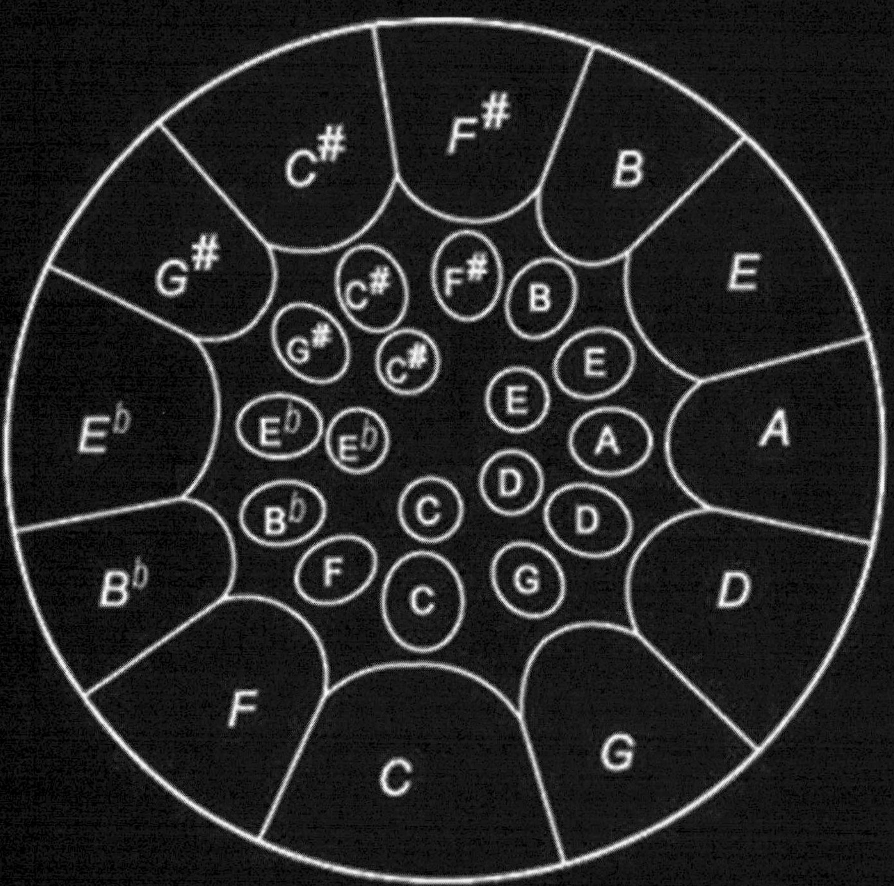

Tenor Pan Notes

John Henrik Clarke

M. WILLIAMS & M. AMALEMBA

BLACK SCIENTISTS & INVENTORS

BOOK 1

AS SEEN ON TV

BLACK WO

SCIENTI

&

NTO

me 1

Written by

Michael Williams

& A.A.D.

Illustrated by:

Cindy Soso

EQUIANO'S EPIGRAMS

THE INTERESTING NARRATIVE IN POETRY

by

JOHN AGARD

ofi

D TO BE A BAD BW

MAIZA AND MASTE

Meets Alexander Miles

The Inventor

www.bispublicatio

FULL PACK 1

BLAC

BLACK SCIENTISTS & INVENTORS
BOOK 2
KWAKU
AND HIS HEARING AID
Written by Darren Meade
Michael Willia
READY STEADY GOLD
Great Olympians
A collection of 13 great Black s
from all over the world. They are pre
with a gold parchment finish, the
Full Pa

Questions & Answers For Michael Williams

1. Why did you decide to write this book?

For at least 15 years I have been researching the contributions that people of African descent have made in terms of science, inventions and innovations. I chose to do this some fifteen years ago simply because being educated as a child and a young adults, I was never taught about the contributions that Africans had made in these areas. I found that in my maths, science and history classes, I only learnt about Europeans that contributed in these areas. I may have learnt a little about the Asian contribution to maths, but nothing about the African. All I was told about the Africans were that they were savages and were civilized by Europeans during the trans-Atlantic Enslavement trade.

Let me also say because we focused on the contributions of Black Scientists & Inventors to the UK, we wanted to find the earliest dates that these contributions were made. It just so happened that these dates did not go back to 50 years or 100 years as some would have us believe, but in fact went back to at least 10, 000 years. I needed to tell the truth and correct this wrong.

2. Why aren't your books in every home and school in the UK?

In terms of schools, I personally don't think that these truths can ever be taught, because they will open a Pandora's box. What do I mean by that? You see the history of Africans is a shared history with Europeans and this history is not all pleasant and does not show the European in a favorable light. Man and civilization started in Africa and then migrated throughout the world we can then easily deduce that the first civilization across the planet was indeed thoseof African people. In the UK history mostly starts with Alfred the Great and William the Conqueror in 1066 CE, you may hear a bit about Roman Briton, If you can answer questions correctly on those three, you'll score an A grade. You will never be taught anything about African Briton, because that preceded all the other three periods. It then connects the dots of who may have built some of the ancient relics that have been found across the UK. And it does not warn of a point that then these ancient people who once built the UK and gave this location civilization, arts, science and culture, would one day (1500s - 1900s CE), be enslave by Europeans, treated worse than animals and even brought over here and put in Human Zoo cages.

3. What makes you qualified to speak on this subject?

I have been researching and studying the subject of Black Scientists and Inventors for more than 15 years and African history in general for much longer. I have been trained in Engineering, computing, electronics and physics. I am of African descent and have experienced many of the things that we have presented in this book.

4. Can you prove any of what you have written in this book?

Yes and no. I say this because we have taken the position that it is for the reader to prove what we have written correct or incorrect and the only way to do this is that they engage in further serious research on this topic. We have used similar methods that western scholars have used to write books on human civilization, inventions and innovations. In regards to living scientists and inventors wherever possible we have interviewed them directly so the facts about them is of a primary source. We then have investigated around the information gained from them in order to corroborate what we have learnt.

5. If what you have written is true, then why don't more people know about it, I mean how comes its not public knowledge?

I think I partially answered this earlier and we certainly answered this in the section on what is a good education. But I will answer it again in this way, by asking you to ask the teachers of the school your child attends why is the information in this book not taught in school? While you are at it you can also ask your local library or bookshop why don't you stock this type of book?

6. Okay now we know this what now, how is this going to improve children's results at school or help young people get a J.O.B?

In one sense this book has not been created to help inspire young people to look for jobs, but instead to inspire and encourage young people to create jobs for themselves and others, by creating there own businesses from their ideas. We hope that in this book the reader is encouraged in the areas of science, inventions and product creation, also acknowledging the struggles Africans have gone through at times in very hostile environments, but have persevered with an indomitable spirit. With this spirit they have given the world its earliest civilizations, its arts, sciences and languages etc. and were the great builders of the pyramids of Egypt, the religious and learning centres of Timbuktu and Churches in Lalibela, towns and cities such as Great Zimbabwe and builders of Stonehenge, yes Stonehenge. If they did it once by reading this book they should know that they can do it again.

7. I think that this book and in fact all the BIS Publications books should be widely available in this country and around the world; how can I help to make that happen?

Inform as many people as possible to the types of cultural educational publications we are producing. Make sure your child's library, school, college or University are stocking our titles. But most of all whether the educational institutions are stocking our titles or not, one way to ensure they go to directly to where they are needed are for you the parents, carers, aunts, uncles and friends to ensure that our titles are on your bookshelves.

Questions & Answers For Manyonyi Amalemba

1. Why did you choose to write this book and why now?

BIS Publications had an original publication of international black scientists mainly Americans and so this was an advancement on the previous editions but with a UK bias.

2. How long did it take to write?

This book has been 2 years [since I've been involved] in the making

3. Why the mixture of subject - science/history/politics etc?

Any topic one chooses to study has to be embedded in history give it purpose and relevance for better understanding of the reader/user.

4. Was the research difficult to do? And if so any examples of difficulties faced?

As most works/books written have mainly been from a European/western perspective, it becomes difficult sieving through in order to get closer to truth.

5. How much help did it need to complete?

We worked basically from the original concept and then sort help when needed especially with the research and the writing and editing from those with interests and that we could trust with such sensitive materials.

6. Why the collaboration with others?

Trust and belief in the final product with the best work possible - we all believed and respect each other and the work.

7. What age group is the book aimed at?

This book is aimed at anyone that feels the need to learn and gain knowledge in order to elevate themselves and be proud of who they are.

8. Can anyone read the book or just for the affected black community?

Anyone from any race, colour or creed can learn something from reading this book.

9. Is the book only relevant for the UK audience?

Not aimed solely to UK audience but an international one as well. 'We are all in this together' - for real and if we don't understand where we have come from then moving forward might prove difficult. The UK bias was due to the fact that most books in this arena are usually written and published from across the pond – USA. Although home grown, the scientists featured have international outlook and achievement.

10. What do you hope to achieve with this books publication?

Hopefully, share and spread the knowledge. There is a running theme in the book of perseverance, endurance, achievement and shared success - following ones dream/ vision. It also shows that with Focus, concentration and determination/belief, our communities can rise to ever dizzier heights towards self-determination and this can only be progressive and positive thing for all concerned.

Bibliography

1. Black Scientists & Inventors Book 1, Ava Henry & Michael Williams, BIS Publications, 1999.

2. Black Scientists & Inventors Book 2, Michael Williams & Ava Henry, BIS Publications, 2003.

3. Black Scientists & Inventors Book 3, Michael Williams, BIS Publications, 2007.

4. Black Women Scientists & Inventors Vol1, Michael Williams & Djehuti Ankh-Kheru, BIS Publications, 2007.

5. Simply The Best, Michael Williams, AAD, Cindy Soso, BIS Publications, 2010.

6. Black Entrepreneurs in the UK, Michael Williams & Cindy Soso, BIS Publications, 2006.

7. Self Publish Successfully: A 20-Step Guide, Michael Williams, BIS Publications, 2013.

8. Valiant Women-Profile Of African Women In Struggle 1500s -1970s, Zindika Kamauesi, BIS Publications, 2010.

9. Ready Steady Gold, Great Olympians, Zindika Kamauesi, BIS Publications, 2012.

10. The A to Z of Parenting – An essential guide to effective parenting, Karlene

11. Rickard, PMEC and BIS Publications, 2006.

12. Black Achievers in the UK, Karlene Rickard , KJ Academy Calendar 2005.

13. Blacks In Science: ancient & modern, Edited by Ivan Van Sertima, Transaction Books, 1983.

14. Message To The People,The Course of African Philosophy, Marcus Garvey, edited by Tony Martin, The Majority Press, 1986.

15. Up From Slavery, Booker T. Washington,

16. African People European Holidays Book One, Rev Ishakamusa Barashango, IVth Dynasty Publishing Company, 1993.

17. African People European Holidays, Book Two, Rev Ishakamusa Barashango, IVth Dynasty Publishing Company,

18. To Shoot Hard Labour, The Life & Times of Samuel Smith an Antiguan workingman 1877-1982, K B. Smith and F C. Smith, Karia Press, 1989.

19. Our Story, A Hand Book of African History And Contemporary Issues, edited by Akyaaba Addai-Sebo & Ansel Wong, London Strategic Policy Unit, 1988.

20. The Hidden Truth Free Your Mind, Exploding The Truth Behind Black History, Investigator (Andrew Muhammad), Hakiki Publishing, 2004.

21. Staying Power, The History of Black People In Britain,
Peter Fryer, Pluto Press.

22. The Sunday Times News Paper,

23. The Jamaica Times, pg 6-7, January 2014.

24. The Windrush Legacy, Memories of Britain's
post-war Caribbean Immigrants,

25. BCA, Edited by Sam Walker and Alvin Elcock,
Black Cultural Archives, 1998.

26. How They Made A Million: The Dyke & Dryden Story,
Tony Wade, Hansib Publication, 2001.

27. New Dimensions In African History, Yosef
ben-Jochannan John Hendrik Clarke, Africa World Press, 1991.

28. Black Inventors: From Africa To America,
CR. Gibbs, Three Dimensional Publishing Company, 1995.

29. Black Inventors, Keith Holmes, Global Black Inventors

30. The ANKH, African Origins of Electromagnetism,
Nur Ankh Amen, Nur Ankh Amen Press, 1993.

31. A History of Black Presence In London, GLC,
Greater London Council, 1986.

32. The Oxford English Minidictionary,
Joyce M. Hawkins, Clarendon Press, 1994

33. The Jewish Phenomenon,
7 Keys To Enduring Wealth Of A People, Steven Silbiger, 2009.

34. New African Magazine, Curtis Abraham, Pg 82 – 87, IC Publication,
August/September 2011.

35. Return To Glory, The Powerful Stirring of the Black Race,
Joel A. Freeman & Don B. Griffin, Treasure House, 2003.

36. Africa's Gift To Britain 2003 Calendar, Michael Williams,
BIS Publications, 2002.

37. Great Jamaican Scientists Book Two, Anthony S. Johnson, Iskamol, 2001.

38. Naming African Role Models (NARM) Highlighting African British
Male Role Models 1907-2007, Kwaku, BTWC, 2010.

39. Re-Membering Africa, Ngugi Wa Thiong'o,
East African Educational Publishers LTD, 2009.

40. The Trader, The Owner, The Slave: Parallel Lives in the Age of Slavery,
James Walvin, Vintage Books, 2008.

41. Making Freedom Exhibition Guide, Arthur Torrington,
Windrush Foundation, 2013.

42. Post Traumatic Slave Syndrome,America's Legacy of Enduring Injury & Healing, Joy Degrury, Uptone Press, 2005.

43. Nile Valley Civilization - Exploding The Myths, Anthony Browder, The Institute of Karmic Guidance, 1992.

44. Changing Generations: Challenging Power & Oppression in Britain Today, Alan Sharp, BIS Publishing Services, 2014.

45. NOI Research Group

46. Encyclopedia Britania,

47. Wikipedia

48. Think & Grow Rich ,A Black Choice, Dennis Kimbro & Napoleon Hill, Ballantine Books, 1991.

49. Out Witting The Devil, Audio Book, Napoleon Hill,

50. The Master Key, C.F. Haanel, Beyond World Publishing, 2008.

51. Motivating & Preparing Black Youth For Success, Jawanza Kunjufu, African American Images, 1986.

52. The Master Key To Riches, Napoleon Hill.

53. Rich Dad Poor Dad, Robert Kiyosaki & Sharon Lechter, Warner Brothers.

54. Getting Black Folks To Sell, George Subria, Very Serious Business Enterprises, 1988.

55. Protecting Your #1 Asset, Michael Lechter, ESQ, Creating Fortunes from Your Ideas, Warner Brothers Books, 1994

56. The Confessions of a Successful Self-Publishing Author, Michael Williams, BIS Publications (To Be Published)
UNESCO - Iron in Africa- revising the History/ww/Africa [unesco.org/en/]
Pitt Rivers Museum, Oxford/University of Oxford

57. www.reshafim.org - ancient Egyptian pottery

58. www.ruperthopskins.com/Agriculture in Africa

59. Saharanvibe.blogspot.co.uk (2008)

60. Ancient Britons Vol 1, David Mac Ritchie, Published 1991, Preston

61. De Erfenis van Zwarte Uitvinders & Wetenschappers, Djehuti-Ankh-Kheru, 2003

62. The Legacy of Black Scientists & Inventors, (English Translation) Djehuti Ankh-Kheru, 2007.

63. Sex And Race
Volume 1, J. A. Rogers, 7th Edition, (Helga M. Rogers), 1967.

Glossary

- **Academic** - scholarly and intellectual, and not vocational or practical
- **Aesthetic** - sensitive to or appreciative of art or beauty
- **Africa** - Is the world's second-largest continent on the earth. It straddles the equator and encompasses numerous climate areas; it is the only continent to stretch from the northern temperate to southern temperate zones. It is recognised as the birth place of modern man.
- **African** - a person referred to as a Moor, Blackamoore, Negro, Bantu, Niolic, Grimaldi etc.
- **A luta Continua** - The struggle continues (Portuguese)
- **[The] Americas** - are the combined continental landmasses of North America and South America along with their associated islands.
- **Apartheid** - a political system in South Africa from 1948 to the early 1990s that separated the different peoples living there and gave privileges to those of European origin.
- **Anti Oxidants** - a substances/agent that prevents oxidation(oxygen infusion)
- **Arthritis** - a medical condition affecting a joint/joints causing pain, swelling & stiffness.
- **Asthma** - a disease of the respiratory system, sometimes caused by allergies
- **Athleticism** - relating to athletics or any other sports activities(sporty)
- **Ausar** - The name the people of Kemet named their God. The Greeks called Osiris.
- **Auset** - The name the people of Kemet named their Goddess and the Greeks called Isis.
- **Barley** - grain from a cereal plant used for malt production
- **B.C.E.** - Before the Common Era

- **Biotech** - use of biological processes for industrial production(food/vaccines)
- **Blackamoors** - People who are referred to as African, Negro or Black
- **Black Jacobins** - A history of the Haitian Revolution of 1793-1804, by CLR James
- **Black Inferiority** - A mind set which has been created from slavery, colonisation and White Supremacy
- **Blog** - online opinion led websites
- **BMA** - British Medical Association
- **Botany** - scientific study of plants
- **Briton Celt** - Indo-European, originating in Germany and France.
- **Briton** - a member of an ancient Celtic people who once lived in southern Britain
- **Britain** - country where Britons reside
- **Britannia** - the personification and symbol of Great Britain, shown as a seated woman wearing a helmet and holding a trident
- **Caribbean** - is a region that consists of the Caribbean Sea, its islands, and the surrounding coasts. The region is south-east of the Gulf of Mexico and the North American mainland, east of Central America, and north of South America.
- **C.E.** - The Common Era
- **Chemotherapy** - the use of chemical agents to treat disease e.g. cancer
- **CM** - Clinical Medicine
- **Colour Bar** - Laws put in place to manage/perpetuate racism in UK
- **Comfort** - state of being comfortable/physically relaxed
- **Conductivity** - ability to transmit heat, electricity & sound
- **Colonisation** - Being terrorized into enslavement in your own country by the another country in order to economically benefit that country.

- **The Colour Bar** - barriers between races
- **Conscious** - fully appreciating the importance of something (thinking/choosing/ perceiving)
- **Cosmetic Dentistry** - dental(teeth related)- improvement /enhancement
- **Creativity** - ability to use the imagination to develop new and original ideas or things
- **Cricket** - outdoor bat and ball game with wickets famous in England
- **Dee Jay(D J)** - presenter of music on media (disc jockey)
- **Desalination** - (de-salting) is a process of removing dissolved salts from water, thus producing fresh water from seawater. Desalting technologies can be used for many applications.
- **Djed** - An ancient Egyptian (Kemetic) symbol meaning 'stability', it is the symbolic backbone of the god Osiris / Ausar.
- **DNA** - is the means by which hereditary characteristics pass from one generation to the next. (deoxyribonucleic acid)
- **Doctorate** - highest level of university degree awarded for producing extensive original research or other high achievements.
- **Drugs** - medicine
- **Dyslexia** - impaired ability to understand written language:
- **Educationally Sub-normal (ESN)** - classification in UK education system referring to students/pupils being well below the considered competency level.
- **Endorphins** - natural pain killers
- **Engineer** - maker/designer/user/contriver of mechanical clever devices
- **Enslaved** - A people(persons) who have been forced into a lifestyle of forced labour for the economic advancement of another. Changing the noun slaves to an adjective enslaved, these individuals are given an identity as people. An enslaved person will have thoughts of freedom, even if all they have known is this enslaved condition.

- **Environment** - all the external factors influencing the life and activities of humans, animals and plants
- **Fascism** - dictatorial movement/centrally controlling private enterprise and represses all opposition under extreme nationalism
- **Free Radicals** - a highly reactive atom or group of atoms with an unpaired electron
- **Geek** - proud to and/or enthusiastic user of computers/other technology
- **Genetics** - study of heredity
- **Genome** - the full compliment of genetic material that an organism inherits from the parents (chromosomes and genes)
- **GMC** - General Medical Council
- **Grammar School** - a state secondary school teaching children who are traditionally selected for high academic ability
- **Hat-trick**- three wins or successes, especially goals.
- **Heptathlon** - Athletic contest with seven events
- **Honours** - official recognition of academic excellence given to students by colleges and universities at graduation
- **HIV / AIDS** - Human Immunodeficiency Virus
- **Human Trafficking** - modern day term for enslavement and trading in humans
- **Iberian Celt** - or Black Celt, crossed over from North Africa into Spain, where they set up a base and then migrated into the British Isle.
- **Immune systems** - system that recognizes and opposes disease
- **Innovative** - new and creative, especially in the way that something is done
- **Instrumentation** - the use of instruments as tools or for measurement or control
- **Invent** - to be the first to think of, make, or use something

- **Kemet** - old name for present day Egypt
- **Lab Technician** - skilled in industrial techniques or the practical application of a science Lazima Tuta Shinda Bila Shaka: Swahili for We shall be victorious - No doubt!.
- **MB** - Bachelor of Medicine
- **Measles** - contagious acute viral disease with symptoms that include a bright red rash of small spots
- **MD** - Medical Doctor
- **Meningitis** - a viral or bacterial infection inflames the meninges, causing symptoms such as severe headaches, vomiting, stiff neck, and high fever
- **Microbiology** - the scientific study of microscopic organisms and their effects
- **MIND** - The one intelligence out of which all that has been created and is sustained.
- **Millenniums** - a period of 1,000 years, especially a period that begins or ends in a year that is a multiple of 1,000
- **Millennia** - a period of 1,000 years, especially a period that begins or ends in a year that is a multiple of 1,000
- **MRCP** - Member of the Royal College of Physicians
- **Mystery Systems** - Thought, Man Know Thy Self.
- **NESTA** - National Endowment for Science, Technology & Arts
- **Neurologist** - studies the nervous system and its treatment thereof
- **Nigeria** - largest of the West African countries - traversed by the Niger river
- **Opportunity** - a chance, especially one that offers some kind of advantage
- **Ophthalmic** - relating to the eyes, or located in the region of the eye
- **Orthopaedics** - concerned with the nature and correction of disorders of the bones, joints, ligaments, or muscles

- **Pan Africanism** - the belief that unity is vital to economic, social, and political progress and aims to "unify and uplift" people of African descent.
- **Physician** - a doctor who diagnoses and treats diseases and injuries using methods other than surgery
- **Poliomyelitis** - a severe infectious viral disease, usually affecting children or young adults, that inflames the brain stem and spinal cord, sometimes leading to loss of voluntary movement and muscular wasting
- **Prejudice** - a preformed opinion, usually an unfavourable one, based on insufficient knowledge, irrational feelings, or inaccurate stereotypes
- **Professional** - relating to or belonging to a profession
- **Racism** - prejudice or animosity against people who belong to other races
- **Renewable** - able to be sustained or renewed indefinitely
- **Research** - methodical investigation into a subject in order to discover facts, to establish or revise a theory, or to develop a plan of action based on the facts discovered
- **Restorative** - tending or meant to give somebody new strength or vigour
- **Revitalisation** - to give new life or energy to somebody or something
- **Scanner** - an input device used to convert an image or text into digital form for storage or display
- **SCEPTRE** - Surrey Centre for Excellence in professional Training to enhance experience
- **Scientist** - somebody who has scientific training or works in one of the sciences
- **Secondary modern** - formerly, a secondary school offering a more practical and less academic education than a grammar school and attended by students who did not pass the eleven-plus exam
- **Serotonin** - acts as a neurotransmitter, constricts blood vessels at injury sites, and may affect emotional states. a chemical derived from the amino acid tryptophan

- **Sickle cell** - a red blood cell that is crescent-shaped as a result of an inherited mutation in the cell's haemoglobin
- **Silures** - an ancient Briton powerful and warlike tribe. According to Roman historian Tacitus's biography of Agricola, the Silures usually had a dark complexion and curly hair.
- **Spectroscopy** - study of spectra, especially to determine the chemical composition of substances and the physical properties of molecules, ions, and atoms
- **Sustainable** - able to be maintained
- **Systems** - a combination of related parts organized into a complex whole
- **Technology** - a method or methodology that applies technical knowledge or tools
- **Telescope** - device for looking at distant objects making them appear nearer.
- **Treatments** - an act of subjecting something to a physical, chemical, or biological process or agent
- **Vaccine** - a preparation containing weakened or dead microbes of the kind that cause a disease, administered to stimulate the immune system to produce antibodies against that disease
- **Virus** - a sub microscopic parasitic particle of a nucleic acid surrounded by protein that can only replicate within a host cell.
- **West Indian** - of Caribbean origin
- **White Supremacy:** (racism) A mind set which creates and governs a system that control all non white's activity. Ie: (economics, education, entertainment, labour, law, politics, religion, sex and war)
- **World war** - a war involving a number of countries on each side, with fighting spread over much of the world

Index

A

B

C

D

E

I

J

K

L

M

N

O

P

Q

R

S

T

U

W

Y

Z

Michael Williams

Michael Williams is the author of several popular children books, which include the best-selling Black Scientists & Inventors series. He develops educational packs / resources which are available in print and electronic media format. In between running one of his publishing companies, he can be seen giving presentations and workshops to both children and adults on the theme of black history and blacks in science.

Manyonyi Amalemba

As a newly published author himself, Manyonyi Amalemba has always loved learning and acquiring knowledge. In comprehending and internalizing it, he believes that 'knowledge must manifest' - words and promises are cheap. His thirst to learn equally from the younger and older, helps him keep his balance and grounding. Manyonyi wishes all that drink from this particular fountain of ours, equally share in order that 'we may all reach our rememberings and reawaken the greatness that we all know is within our genes. Remember the spirit of our ancestors - nothing is impossible just challenging and we need these challenges in order to grow.' Manyonyi Amalemba (co-Author)

Notes

Notes

Notes

#0038 - 180516 - C0 - 210/148/20 - PB - DID1457003